The ADAM and JOE Book

ADAM BUXTON AND JOE CORNISH

READER ADVISORY
HIGH DENSITY
WARNING

4 BOOKS

WORLD OF WONDER

CW00764850

MACMILLAN

First published in 1999 by Channel 4 Books, an imprint of Macmillan Publishers Ltd, 25 Eccleston Place, London SW1W 9NF, Basingstoke and Oxford.

www.macmillan.co.uk

Associated companies throughout the world.

ISBN 0 7522 1330

Text © Adam Buxton and Joe Cornish, 1999

The right of Adam Buxton and Joe Cornish to be identified as the authors of this work has been asserted by them in accordance with the Copyright, Designs and Patents Act 1988.

All rights reserved. No part of this publication may be reproduced, stored in or introduced into a retrieval system, or transmitted, in any form, or by any means (electronic, mechanical, photocopying, recording or otherwise) without the prior written permission of the publisher. Any person who does any unauthorized act in relation to this publication may be liable to criminal prosecution and civil claims for damage.

10 9 8 7 6 5 4 3 2 1

A CIP catalogue record for this book is available from the British Library.

Design by Dan Newman/Perfect Bound Design and Adam Buxton

Credits
Derek Askem (photography): pp 22–23, 52 *bottom*, 72–74
Julia Hember (photography): pp 10–13, 14, 16 *main*, 19, 29, 50 *top left*, 59, 62, 63, 70 *top and bottom*, 71 *top and bottom*, 82 *bottom*, 84, 85, 86, 87, 94
Tim Ridley (photography): pp 36–37, 44–45
Zac Sandler (illustrations): pp56–57
Shaun Whiteside (transposer): pp 15, 58, 75
Colour reproduction by Speedscan
Printed by Milanostampa

This book is sold subject to the condition that it shall not, by way of trade or otherwise, be lent, re-sold, hired out, or otherwise circulated without the publisher's prior consent in any form of binding or cover other than that in which it is published and without a similar condition including this condition being imposed on the subsequent purchaser.

The Adam and Joe Show is a World of Wonder production.
Executive producers: Fenton Bailey and Randy Barbato
Series producer: Debbie Searle

ADAM & JOE'S MASQUERADE
This book could win you a day with Adam & Joe!
Hidden in the illustrations in this book are twenty cryptic clues which lead to an actual location somewhere in the UK, where Adam & Joe have stripped naked, painted themselves gold and buried themselves in a small crate. Once you've examined the book thoroughly and deciphered the clues, hurry to the location and start digging. Adam and Joe may well have forgotten to provide themselves with food, breathing holes, or telly. The first reader to dig them up will win an exciting afternoon with the little-known comedy duo, including the chance to rush them to a lavish private hospital and pay their medical bills, should they still be alive. Let the Masquerade begin!

THE CONTENTS OF THIS BOOK

Front cover (unsuitable for use as roach material)
Rear cover (displays lies to make you buy book)
Spine (displays title for easy identification when on shelf)
Corners (can be used for cleaning beneath fingernails)
Edges (provide ventilation and access for viewing pages)

Ken Korda's Movie Guides (cut out and keep if you're insane)
Ken Korda's History of the Movies (history will teach us nothing, as Sting once so wisely sang)
Rules of the Cinema (previously unwritten laws now written)

Vinyl Justice Museum (entry free except for students, OAPs and unemployed)
More Vinyl Justice (compilation guidelines and top ten albums and that)

Guide to Successful Street Spitting (it's a gooba-licious loogie-rama)
Useless CV Guide (it's your CV that's useless, not our guide)
Guide to Street Scoring (designed to generate controversy and free publicity)
Guide to Serial Killing (not intended for use by actual serial killers)
Boring Meal Survival Guide (printed on special wipe-clean laminated paper)
Guide to Lending Protocol (examine before lending book to mates)
Guide to Dancing (we've seen you dancing and we you know you need it)
Guide to Bath Traumas (dip in before you dip in)
Guide to Exam Cheating (don't blame us if you fail)
Guide to being Home Alone (no, it's not all about wanking)
Guide to Record Stores (with useless maps and things)

TOP

REAR

FRONT

Toytanic: The Script (Part One)
Toytanic: The Script (Part Two)
The Toy Patient (you know – for kids!)
The Making of Saving Private Ryan (you'll wish they hadn't)
Hot New Gits (fluffy future stars you'll want to stuff)

Clash of the Hogans (it's a Hogan explogan!)
Bobo! The Bob Hoskins Story (he paid us to put this in)

The Robert De Niro Calypso (he's a loverly pers-juan, and a very good actor)
The Footie Song (ball ball ball, footie footie footie!)
My Name is Roscoe (because speed equals distance over time)

Build your own A&J bedroom (only habitable if you're very very tiny)
Steal These Pranks! (or alternatively just ignore them)
A&J Series Guide (completist's guide to every episode ever broadcast)
Dear Baad Dad (yes, he really is Adam's dad, and yes he really wrote this)
Dr. Fischer Verlag's Encyclopaedia of Partial Medicine (useless advice on spots, mental health and wanking)
Louise's Page (guess what he likes?)

Sweets of the Future (researched using time machine)
Wankst Letters Page (densely packed random bullshit)
A&J's Stand-Up Diary (pop-up stand-up diary in Japanese edition only)
English Literature Exam paper (ideal revision material for those happy to fail)

Plus literally 12 other pages of stuff there isn't room to tell you about!

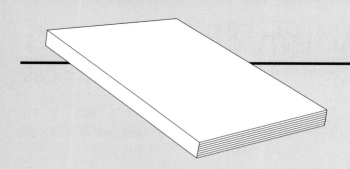

INSTRUCTIONS

WELCOME TO THE ADAM & JOE BOOK

Thank you for purchasing the Adam & Joe Book. Before operating your new book, please study these instructions thoroughly. They will help you to become familiar with your book and its functions, and to obtain years of trouble-free performance.

WHAT IS A BOOK?

Books are a revolution in home entertainment technology. Each book is filled with dozens of pages, all filled from top to bottom with different words and writing. Reading these words causes images and ideas to form in the user's head, almost as if there is a television inside their brain. Incredibly, books require no power source, are fully portable and can be used again and again.

CAUTION

While reading certain passages, some people may experience dizziness, motion sickness, nausea or boredom. If you or your child experience any of these symptoms, discontinue use immediately.

IMPORTANT!

Do not attempt to repair, re-write or disassemble this book. Doing so invalidates your guarantee. There are no user-serviceable parts inside. Refer to qualified servicing personnel only.

Contents may settle in transit. Some gaps in logic are normal in products of this kind.

GETTING STARTED

Remove all packaging from your book, including the various price reduction stickers.

BASIC OPERATIONS

1. Hold your book in both hands and raise it up in front of your face, or lower your face towards the book.
2. Grasp the first page (or 'cover') between thumb and forefinger at its outside edge and rotate it gently around the spine until resistance is felt.
3. Now simply point your eyes at the word at the top left of the page thus revealed on the left.
4. Continue to 'read' each word on the page, one at a time, working from left to right and then from top to bottom.
5. When you reach the end of the words on a page, turn it over and continue on the next page.
6. Continue until bored, or there are no more words.

Literary Information

		Per page	%RDA
Words	63,258	658	42
Syllables	345,564	3,675	53
Verbs	10,337	1,299	76
of which adverbs	4,701	512	72
Adjectives	9,024	980	56
Nouns	11,422	1,256	100
of which pronouns	347	45	87
Swearwords	3245	355	120
Errors and lies	17	0.27	3

Adam & Joe Book

SPECIFICATIONS

ISBN 0671-03387-0
Height: 246mm Width: 189 mm Depth: 9 mm
Printed four-colour web offset litho, perfect bound
Contents: paper, glue, ink, varnish
Weight when shipped: 388g

TROUBLESHOOTING

If you experience any of the following difficulties while using the book, use the troubleshooting guide below to help remedy the problem.

PROBLEM	SOLUTION
The book will not open!	Check you are opening the book on the correct side. The book will not open along the bound edge. Check you have not glued the pages together.
Words and pictures are blurred!	Check you are wearing your reading glasses. Try adjusting the distance between your eyes and the book.
There are no words or pictures on the pages at all!	Tilt book away from glare of bright light. Check you have not mistaken a ream of blank paper or piece of polystyrene for the book.
The words and images are upside-down!	Check you are holding the book the correct way up. The bound edge should be on your left with the front cover facing you.
The book appears to be about amateur nude photography!	Check you have not picked up an amateur nude photography book by accident. Many books appear similar, always inspect the cover carefully before use.
There is no sound!	This is a book, and as such is not designed to make noises.
The book is not funny!	Check you are slightly off your tits and do not have a sophisticated sense of humour.

We take every care to ensure this product reaches you in perfect condition. However, if the contents are unsatisfactory please send the whole back cover with the Best Before date visible and a sample of the contents to someone you don't know at a randomly chosen address from off the telly. They'll probably be able to sort you out, no worries. Don't blame us and anyway, we've moved. Sorry.

A&J 7

HOT NEW GITS

NEXT! PLEASE

NITME
The poodle you want to stuff

Age: 29

You've seen her in: *Toytrainspotting* as the sherbet-addicted Sick Toy, and *Showtoys* as a filthy lapdancing poodle who'll stop at nothing to show people her tits. She also starred in one of 28000 *Flat Eric* parodies back in 1999.

You'll be seeing her in: *Oh Carol! – The Carol Vorderman Story* coming this month to The Vorderman Channel. She plays Toby Anstis from Children's BBC.

The story so far: "I wanted to be the greatest actress in the history of this shitfilled dogburger we call Earth, and when I saw a documentary about the 90s soap star Martine McCutcheon, I knew I could be. I decided to try for a part in *Eastendtoys* as it seemed easy, just shouting and whining. I saw an opening, went right up and sniffed it and now I am famous and attractive."

But the transition from soap dog to gritty film bitch was tough on the young Nitme and she found herself involved in a number of bizarre and sometimes hilarious projects before becoming a regular in *The Adam & Joe Show.* "Yeah, that was a weird time. Actually there's a very funny story about that which I can't remember."

Since leaving Channel 4's homemade crapfactory she has done almost nothing. "I can't get motivated unless someone actually picks me up and shakes me, or puts thread on my arms or sticks a coathanger up my bumhole. Also I am large and difficult to control and my head tends to flop about." However, it was exactly these qualities that landed her a role in the promo for *Sweet Johnny* by the Welsh band Gorky's Zygotic Mynci. She was cast as Alex James, the louche booze-based bass player from the mockney band Blur, in an hilarious recreation of their Song 2 promo. *Sweet Johnny* propelled the Gorkys to the bottom of the charts and they swore never to work with Nitme again.

So when's The Carol Vorderman Story on?: To be honest, I made that up to make her look more busy than she really is, 'cos her agent promised me tickets to *Can't Cook Won't Cook* if I did. **Oh.**

Mmm... drugs. Nitme in *Toytrainspotting*.

KATE WILTENS
She's posh and wet, but feisty also

Age: 4

You've seen her in: *Toytanic* as Rose the piglet who bares all for the filthy minded Leonardo Di Crapio. You may also have caught her in the irritating lawyer-based television hit, *Ally McSqueal*. She played Ally's romantic nemesis and blonde cypher Georgia Porgia.

You'll be seeing her in: *A Gift Of Monkeys*, a lush screen adaptation of Francis Fundle's classic tale of loss and monkeys featuring the frilly period dress stylings of Janine Louche. It's the twenty-eighth adaptation of the book in the last ten years and promises to be every bit the same as the others, but with different people. Mainly.

The story so far: Discovered singing and dancing in her room by her father, the director and money enthusiast Sir David Frigg-Wiltens at the tender age of 3. He was so impressed with her abilities he hired her on the spot to star opposite Lenny Henry in his remake of *In Bed With Madonna*. Kate's moving rendition of the classic 'bottle fellatio' scene caught the eye of her father, Sir David Frigg-Wiltens, who was directing the film at the time. He was so impressed he cast her on the spot for his next film, *Yentl, The Return*.

What's next then? "I'm working on a documentary for the BBC about poor people and what their lives are actually like. It's been amazing seeing some of the places they sleep. Absolutely tiny and smelly. Some don't even have houses! I envy them in a way, being able to go where they want and do what they want, as long as it doesn't cost any money of course. So liberating! They are such proud people. Many of them can sing, not well, but with such enthusiasm!"

It must have been bacon' in the cabin, but stripping for a pork seems a bit rasher. What?

PORKY O'ROURKE
Don't mention Kevin Bacon

Age: 18

You've seen him in: *Toytrainspotting* as Runton, *Seven Dwarves* as Brad Pigg, *Stuffed Trek: The Toy Generation* as Captain Jean Pork Pighard and in the *Sweet Johnny* promo as Gamon Albarn.

That sounds like typecasting: "Its tough having people come up to you in the street and call you a pig, but I've worked out a fairly devastating put-down that stops them in their tracks. I say 'P.I.G. stands for Pretty Intelligent Person.' After that they realise that it was me and not them that was holding all the cards."

So where's he been?: "My roles have always been quite physically demanding, which I like, but around about the time we were doing *Stuffed Trek* I started to notice quite a lot of my stitches were loose and a large part of my scalp had come away, exposing the fluff beneath it. It wasn't a problem for that shoot as I was playing Patrick Stewart, but since then I've tried to take it a lot easier."

Why is he in this piece then? Good question, as Runton has now retired completely and has no projects of any kind in development. He's not even involved with the internet.

So why the piece then? I don't know, just something to fill up space I suppose. Stop shouting at me. Who are you anyway?

I'm VOICE OF THE READER, a lame device enabling journalists turn two or three miserable informational nuggets into a whole piece. You sound like a know-it-all ponce to me.

Because I am. Oh then.

Is that all? Oh piss off.

Runton as Brad Pigg, unaware that his wife is about to lose her head. Lose her head! Ha.

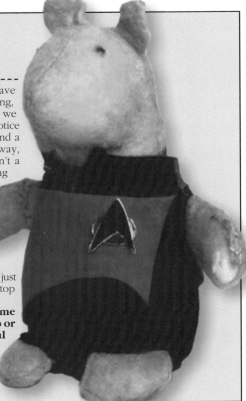

ADAM & JOE'S

STAND-UP DIARY

Like most successful professional comedians, Adam & Joe spent their early years honing their craft in Britain's unforgiving comedy clubs. In these extracts from their tour diaries, they give us a unique look at their struggle with the harsh realities of the stand-up circuit.

Our first public performance at Bromley's premiere amateur stand-up night as 'Springwater & Pasty'. This is the gateway to the South London Pub circuit. Win tonight, and tomorrow we could be top of the bill at the Dog and Duck in Peckham. That's right; when it happens, it happens that fast.

We open with our 'What on earth happens to all those odd socks that vanish in the washing machine?' routine. The audience have never heard anything like it, and they love it. Suddenly we're totally relaxed, and start to riff on the idea that there might be some kind of parallel universe populated by single smelly socks. The audience go wild and, incredibly, we win.

'HA FUCKING HA' AT THE DOG AND DUCK, PECKHAM RYE, OCTOBER '95

This is gonna be a tough one. Hecklers at HFH are notorious. Have changed our name to 'Buxom & Hornish'. We open with our new 'Why do bloody buses all come at once?' routine. It's like magic – the crowd are in the palm of our hands. We segue into our 'Where the hell are all these road cones coming from, maybe they're actually aliens trying to take over the world?' routine and slam it home with our 'Why do women spend so long in the loo, what the hell is it they're doing in there?' turn. We've never heard applause like this before – stand up really is the new rock and roll!

'THE BIG FISH MOON BANANA COMEDY BOX', CAMDEN TOWN, APRIL '96

Sunday night at the Big Fish Moon Banana Comedy Box. This is where the big agents come to scout new talent. Make 'em laugh here, and we've got a shot at the big time. Have changed our name to 'Reverend Spoon and the Man with the Hat', and have decided to try out our new 'Ambassador's Reception' routine, a brilliantly surreal word-for-word

Mention one of these words or themes in your gag, and you're guaranteed to get a laugh every time!

- The Millennium Dome (What a ridiculous waste of money!!!)
- Peter Mandleson (He's gay you know!)
- The Spice Girls (Ha ha ha! They're stupid and they're everywhere!)
- Viagra (The pill that gives you a stiffy!)
- Monica Lewinsky (Loves cigars, but not in her mouth!!!!)
- The Teletubbies (One of them looks gay you know!)
- Windscale (Erm, forgotten what this means...)
- Gus the Gorilla (Gorillas and monkeys are always funny)
- Michael Jackson (he used to be black, now he's white! And also plastic surgery)
- Cherie Blair (She's married to Tony Blair & looks funny! Ha ha ha ha!)
- The Artist Formerly Known As Prince (Imagine what you'd be called!)
- Feng Shui (You know, ha ha ha!)
- Nescafé Ads (They're awful aren't they!)
- Plus – anything out of that day's papers.

re-enactment of the Ferrero Rocher advert.

We follow it up with our Retro Kids' TV routine: 'Did Captain Pugwash really have Seaman Stains? And was Dylan on *The Magic Roundabout* just stoned the whole time?' All it takes is a final; 'Your excellency, you spoil us!' and the place goes wild. Five messages on the answering machine when we get home, all from agents. Get pissed out of heads to celebrate.

THE CRESTA 'IT'S FROTHY MAAAN!' COMEDY AWARD, EDINBURGH, JULY '96

We've been working for this for years, and at last it's happened. The Cresta Comedy Award is headline news and if you win you're pretty much guaranteed a TV show. We can't believe we've made the short-list. Our new name is 'The Jan Leeming Encounter'. The crowd is cold, full of critics and competitors. We launch into our 'Why don't

those chocolate vending machines on underground platforms ever work?' skit. The laughs build to applause, as we improvise on the idea that they've been put there by aliens to test our intelligence. Finally we drive it home with 'And why does the nutter on the bus always sit next to me? What am I, some kind of nutter magnet!?!' We leave feeling pessimistic. We could have been better. The next morning, we discover – we

won it!!!!! And at the awards ceremony a TV producer offers us our very first line of cocaine. Woah! This stuff's fantastic! This is the best night of our lives!

'THE SATURDAY STAND-UP SAUSAGE MACHINE' CHANNEL FIVE TELEVISION, AUG '96

Channel Five, an exciting new TV station promising to lead the way in cutting edge comedy, have offered us a slot on their new weekly topical stand-up showcase. Have changed our name on advice to 'Adam & Joe's Topical Paradise' and will use the show to try our hand at political material. We've picked our targets carefully; Honest John Major, the single currency, alco-pops and the National Lottery. Before the

shoot the producer offers us more cocaine, or 'power-powder' as he calls it. He says it'll make us even sharper and funnier. And boy is he right! We feel really buzzed and totally confident, and new ideas flow out. Wonder how we can get hold of more?

ADAM & JOE'S EARLY TV APPEARANCES

'Stand-Up And Be Counted' – Paramount Comedy Channel, June '96
'The Great Big Stand-Up Showdown' – Sky TV, July '96
'Stand-Up Virgin Stand-ups' Channel 5, Aug '96
'The Saturday Stand-Up Sausage Machine' – Channel 5, Aug '96
'Stand-Up For Yourself' – Channel 4, Aug '96
'Simply Stand-Up' – Channel 4, Aug '96
'The Stand-Up Comedy Experimentation Bunker' – BBC2, October '96
'Stand@Up.Com' – BBC2, December '96
'Stand-Up For Stand-Ups' (In aid of unemployed stand-ups) February '97
'Have I Read Newspapers For This!' – BBC2, April '97
'I Think I'll Turn Over' – BBC1, May '97

FREE cut-out-and-keep
BABY MOVIE MARATHON
by KENNETH KORDA

Pop into your local Bollockbusters with this list in hand, invite some mates round, grab some beers, phone a pizza and enjoy a night of classic baby movies, selected by film expert Ken Korda!

THREE MEN AND A BABY

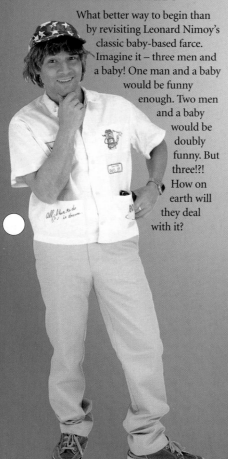

What better way to begin than by revisiting Leonard Nimoy's classic baby-based farce. Imagine it – three men and a baby! One man and a baby would be funny enough. Two men and a baby would be doubly funny. But three!?! How on earth will they deal with it?

Men are hopeless with babies! As if this provocative scenario isn't enough, three of Hollywood's top leading men essay the lead roles. Bang – Selleck! Splam! – Danson! Kaboom – Guttenburg! A cast made in movie heaven in an idea that must have had executives fisting each other with their chequebooks! Watch out for the magical moment when the tiny baby shits itself then pisses all over Danson. A timeless classic.

BABY BOOM

Two of the most powerful words in the cinema lexicon; 'boom' and 'baby' are combined to form one of the most compelling film titles ever. This is an ideal movie for naive young girls who think they can succeed as businesswomen and avoid having babies. Diane Keaton is one of Hollywood's most intelligent, beautiful and talented young actresses, and the only thing this film lacks is a scene in which the baby shits itself and pisses all over her. This however is a tiny fault in an otherwise perfect movie. Enjoy!

BABY'S DAY OUT

It took a filmmaker of genius to realise that the world of baby movies was missing an action adventure story. That filmmaker was the founder of modern cinema, John Hughes, and the movie is Baby's Day Out. Baby-lovers will be breathless with excitement as kidnapped baby 'Binky' escapes in New York pursued by comedy mobsters. Seamless blending of robot babies, real babies and tiny dwarves creates many heart-stopping moments of infant peril. Ten babies were killed during the making of this masterpiece, but it was well worth it. Marvellous.

BABY... SECRET OF THE LOST LEGEND

Not strictly a baby movie, as the story involves a young couple who discovering a baby dinosaur, not a baby person. However, if you scrunch your eyes up it's easy to pretend the dinosaur is a small green child. And if you scrunch your eyes up even more, it's even easier to imagine it shitting itself then pissing all over beautiful Sean Young. Highly entertaining.

THE BABY OF MACON

Peter Greenaway is a visionary genius and one of the most confusing and intensely boring filmmakers working in cinema today. The news that he was to make a baby-based film sent shockwaves of excitement through the baby-movie-loving world. The finished work is no disappointment. At one point a single shot of the baby is held for over half an hour while fat naked men sing in Greek. A masterpiece.

SHE'S HAVING A BABY

What better way to close your baby-movie-marathon than with John Hughes' 1988 tour-de-farce. Hollywood's holy trinity Bacon, Baldwin and McGovern turn in the best performances of their careers as the man who's marrying the woman who's having a baby, a man who knows the man who's marrying the woman who's having the baby, and the woman who's actually going to have the baby. A better title would of course have been *She's Had a Baby, it's just shat itself and now it's Pissing on Her.* I'm going now, byeee!

BOLLOCKBUSTERS

SING-A-LONG WITH ADAM & JOE! Adam & Joe are proud to present the words and music to some of their best-loved songs. So why not grab your guitar or a piano, gather some friends together and have your very own Adam & Joe singalong? (Don't answer that, it's rhetorical.)

Chorus:
My name is Roscoe
That's Roscoe H Spellgood
I like to go a long way in a short time
That's why I increase
My velocity when possible
Cos speed equals distance over time

Well I pulled up by a railroad track
Oh I never saw such a daybreak
The sun was burstin' high over the land
I could hardly see the sky
For the tears in my eyes
And I knew I'd never see my home again

Chorus

Can you hear the pounding of my heart
Well it cuts me like the combine
Harvester I rode in Autumn time
Well the seasons come and go
First the Springtime then the snow
Oh my Mima maybe one day you'll be mine

Chorus

There's a theory that I use
As I hitch-hike down the highway
To calculate how far you are from me
It concerns hypotenuse
And a man who sings the blues
Guess it all comes down to relativity

Chorus

Oooooh.

A&J'S GUIDE TO BEING...
HOME ALONe

Are you a teenager or a retarded twenty-something who still lives with your parents? Are they going away for the night, leaving you to your own devices? Can't you be arsed to invite mates round or throw a party? Then why not take full advantage of your solitary freedom with our activity guide to being home alone.

GET PISSED UP ON YOUR PARENT'S BOOZE

As soon as the front door closes behind them, raid your parent's booze cabinet and get yourself nice and tipsy. Now you're ready to begin your night of domestic abuse.

WARNING: Be sure to pencil mark the fluid level before you drink, then top up with water/tea/ribena depending on substance consumed.

EXPLORE YOUR FAMILY HISTORY

Rifle through your parent's drawers and cupboards looking for evidence of their secret lives. Be prepared to discover your dad's sixties porno mags (usually concealed beneath the lining paper of his shirt drawer), your mum's diary (detailing your mum/dad's infidelity and their near divorce), and evidence that they are still having sex together (oh sweet Jesus).

WARNING: Always replace what you've found exactly where you found it, or your parents won't be able to look you in the eye ever again.

GO NUDIST

Close all the curtains, turn the lights out on the stairs and go naked for the evening. Enjoy letting it all hang out in rooms that haven't seen you nude since you were three years old. Examine your body in every mirror in the house, then arrange multiple mirrors to inspect cracks you've never before set eyes on.

WARNING: Check all wall-mounted mirrors for concealed video cameras before proceeding. You never know.

WALLOW IN NOSTALGIA

Hold a personal retrospective of your own life. Gather all your parent's photo albums, every pathetic painting, clay model and mother's day card your mum ever saved from your childhood. Now examine it all carefully and let the memories of happier days come flooding back. When you find yourself moved to tears by how wonderful you were, your work is done.

WARNING: Do not do this more than once annually, or you risk making yourself permanently suicidally depressed.

TRY EXPERIMENTAL MASTURBATION

Tonight's the night to push your programme of auto-erotic experimentation to new limits. You'll be amazed at how uninhibited you can be with yourself when you know your parents aren't in the next room. Ever wondered if you can pleasure yourself orally, for instance? Been tempted to enjoy yourself alfresco in the in the garden? Or felt the urge to arrange cushions into the shape of your favourite fantasy partner and making sweet love to them? Now's the time to make your wildest dreams come true.

WARNING: Make sure all pets are secured in a locked room before proceeding. They'll only look at you and put you off, or even worse, try to join in.

ENJOY WATER SPORTS

Tired of always locking the door when you use the bathroom? Why not find out what it's like to live in a world without toilet shame. Take a long crap with the door wide open, while singing an improvised song entitled 'everybody look at me I'm having a shit'. Now use every extension cable in the house and rig up your TV, video, hi-fi and games console beside the bath and have the greatest wallow of your life.

WARNING: Water and electricity do not mix, but at least you'll die with a smile on your face.

SCARE YOUR TITS OFF

See if you can make yourself as scared as you were when you were eight and you saw a video nasty for the first time. Rent several grim slasher films or documentaries about ghosts or UFOs, or just tape a couple of editions of Crimewatch. Turn all the lights out and watch them all alone. You'll know you've succeeded in freaking yourself out when you find yourself too terrified to make the journey to your own lavvy, and wind up using a bottle or bowl instead.

WARNING: If you get too frightened, simply switch over to The Open University and you'll soon bring yourself back down to earth.

HOLD A SOLO DISCO

Put on your favourite crappy dance record, clear a space in the living room and let the spirit of Legs & Co possess you. For once you can be totally uninhibited about your taste in music and your bizarre dancing. Why not prop the largest mirror in the house up against a wall and watch yourself groove? Hey, you look great! Now why not imagine you're Martin Fry circa 1985 performing the whole of 'Lexicon of Love' live at the Hammersmith Odeon? Can you make it all the way through the album without disappointing your imaginary audience? I can! Not that I ever actually did that, of course.

WARNING: Do not attempt to do the splits like Prince. When the ambulancemen take you away you will have a hard job explaining what you were doing.

Cracker Jokes

This year why not celebrate the birthday of Little Baby Jesus (or LBJ) by giving an unexpected twist to the absolute best part of Christmas: Crackers! With Adam & Joe's Cracker Page it couldn't be easier! Just photocopy the page and cut out the special Adam & Joe cracker jokes then stick them in your crackers for an extra wonky Cringle treat or something. Imagine the fun! Oh go on, please imagine the fun.

Q: WHERE DO ELEPHANTS PACK THEIR LUGGAGE WHEN THEY GO FOR A DRIVING HOLIDAY?
A: No, not in their trunk, it's nothing to do with their trunks. I meant where do they do the actual packing, and the answer is 'in their bedroom or front room'.

Q: What do they call Mars Bars on Mars?
A: Shazz–winkle Bars.

You'd think that ducks would have learned to stop sitting around quite so much and get out of the way a bit more.

Q: How do astronauts go to the loo?
A: They have a suction funnel for number ones, and I think some kind of extractor tube for number twos but I'm not sure.

Patient: Doctor doctor, I'm think I'm having a heart attack!
Doctor: Why, what makes you think that?
Patient: I've got shooting pains up my left arm and agonising cramps in my chest and I can't breathe!
Doctor: Is this a joke? Oh come on, don't waste my time.

A man walks into a bar with a lion. A lady at the bar screams and runs into the toilet, along with several other customers. Trembling, the bartender asks the man what he is doing with a lion in the bar but the man just orders a beer and sits down. The lion growls but stays calm. The man is finishing his beer when the police arrive. The man explains he thought it would be funny to bring the lion into the bar. He is taken away. So is the lion.

Q: WHAT DO PIRATES CALL THEIR BEST CUTLERY?
A: LONG-JOHN-SILVERWARE.
THAT'S ACTUALLY TRUE.

Q: What do you give a ghost for Christmas?
A: Anything but mints, they hate mints. Socks or chocolates are a safe bet.

Matt Goss: Oh when, will I, will I be famous?
Luke Goss: I can't answer, I can't answer that.
Craig: What?

Child: Mummy, mummy, are we half way there yet?
Mother: About another hour darling.
Child: But you said that an hour ago...
Mother: Quiet darling, Mummy needs to concentrate!
Child: Jesus!

A PENGUIN IN A REVOLVING DOOR
What was the question again?

I'm sure glad I don't work at that Rumourmill. All that overtime, and I've heard they don't even get paid that well.

One day Kev gets a phone call informing him that his ex-flatmate Jimmy Wankbreak, has won the lottery jackpot. Kev immediately starts phoning round, trying to track him down. After a whole morning of calls Kev finally gets the number of Jimmy's office. Kev dials the number and the phone is answered by a young man. "Have you got a Jimmy Wankbreak there?" he asks. "You what?" says the man. "Wankbreak, have you got a Wankbreak there?" says Kev. "Wankbreak?!" says the man. "We don't even get a flipping tea break!"

Boyfriend: What's the matter?
Girlfriend: Nothing.
Boyfriend: Well, something's the matter, what is it?
Girlfriend: If you don't know, then that's half the problem.
Boyfriend: What??!

Q: What do you call the mathematical measure for the amount someone exaggerates?
A: Their exaggeratio.

What's the difference between Diet Pepsi and Pepsi Max? And why does Diet Pepsi from a can taste totally different to Diet Pepsi from a small plastic bottle? Does anyone know?

WHAT'S THE DIFFERENCE BETWEEN A CHICKEN? ONE OF ITS LEGS IS BOTH THE SAME.
THAT CAN'T BE RIGHT CAN IT? SORRY, THERE'S BEEN A MISTAKE.

PROPER JOKE
What do you call a writer who stretches the truth? JOURNELASTIC!
Well, it *sounds* like a joke. I didn't say it would be funny. *You* make some up if you think it's so very easy.

THE VINYL JUSTICE MUSEUM

Good morning/afternoon/evening, sir/madam/sonny/love (delete as applicable). As officers of the Vinyl Justice Squad, we wage an unending war against filthy music crime. Over the years we've gathered a disturbing collection of pop-related criminal memorabilia, or 'disturbo-pop-criminabilia', a selection of which we're proud to make available for public viewing here for the first time ever. Let these artifacts be a warning to you cocky young pop performers who think you're above the law.

EXHIBIT A

As many of you will already know, the world famous Vengabus was recently involved in a high speed crash while travelling southbound on the A3. The bus was fully loaded with Vengaboys when the accident occurred, and Vinyl Justice officers were first on the scene to assist the injured. Even while drugged up to the eyeballs in intensive care, the boys' musical genius remained undiminished, and they wrote these moving lyrics about the disaster.

The Vengabus is coming
The boys on board are bumming
Each other up the plumbing
It's really quite becoming

The Vengabus is swerving
The road ahead is curving
Their driving is disturbing
The wheels mounting the curbing

The Vengabus is crashing
The windows are all smashing
The boys on board are bleeding
They shouldn't have been speeding

The Vengabus has blown up
The boys inside have thrown up
They'll do no more recording
The public are applauding...

Buy rhyming dictionary!

Must must MUST try and learn third chord this week!

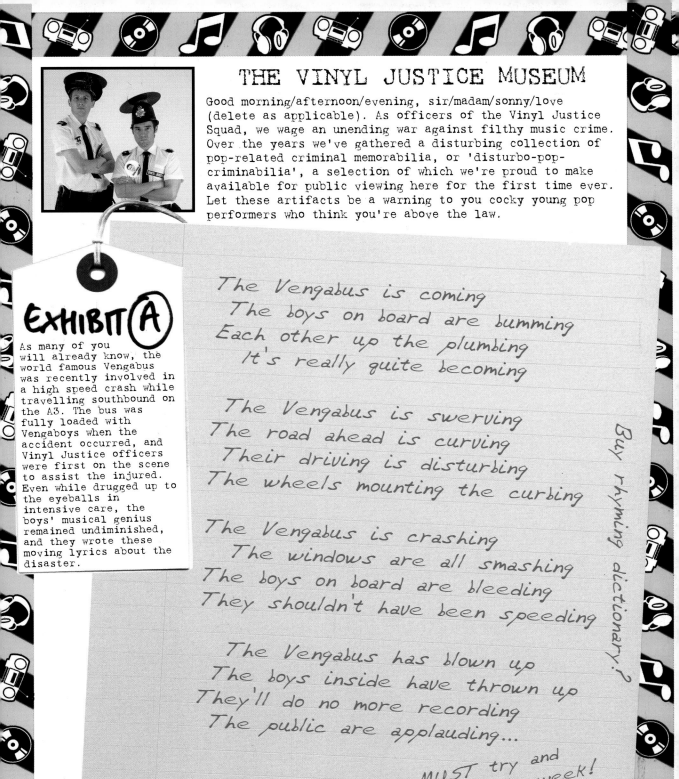

EXHIBIT B

When International rock superstar Lenny Kravitz came to London to play a series of sell-out dates, Vinyl Justice officers took the opportunity to raid his hotel room and seize his property, for no particular reason other than the fact that we felt like knocking him around a bit. Amongst the materials confiscated were these notes Kravitz had made for his new single, which would surely have been a huge hit, had we not intervened.

Buy more tiny leather vests!!

*** Focus marketing on German under-tens who don't speak English

NOTE: Tuesday, 2pm Appointment to have brain pierced.
Remember to ask if it's possible/practical to have both buttocks pierced with a giant brass ring?

GREAT IDEA for new jam on groove similar to 'Fly away'

I want to write a song
A sing-along
Three minutes long
But I am a dong

I want to have a hit
That isn't shit
But I cannot do it
I'm a silly git

oh I want to have ideas
I need some new ideas
Yeah yeah yeah

oh I want to make some cash
I need to make some cash
Yeah yeah yeah

I just bought some shades
And some groovy suedes
I've done my hair in braids
Like in an old decade

If only I could sing
Do the Hendrix thing
Then I'd be king
With my nipple ring

oh I want to show my chest
Look at my sweaty breasts
Yeah yeah yeah

oh I want to think a thought
I want to have a thought
Yeah yeah yeah

EXHIBIT ©

While out shopping in Streatham, London's premiere soft-soul singer/songwriter Des'ree had her handbag cruelly snatched. Said bag contained Des'ree's notebook, in which she jotted ideas for new songs. Miraculously, the discarded bag was later recovered by Vinyl Justice officers. Although a fiver, ten Silk Cut Ultra Mild and a box of Lillets had been stolen, to the relief of pop fans around the world, the notebook remained untouched. The ignorant criminal is no doubt kicking himself even now, as Des'ree's notebook has recently been valued at well over one pound fifty.

Idea for new song: 'Things' (Sung to tune similar to but OH SO SLIGHTLY DIFFERENT from 'Life')

TO DO:
- Have another hit
- Make songs more bland
- Buy food and clothes
- Fin'd ne'w plac'es for apo'stroph'es

Things,
Oooh things,
Oooh thii-iiings,
Oooh things,
Oh things.

***REMEMBER: Help advertise cars and destroy planet.

Things are all over the place,
They take up lots of space,
Some are big and some are small,
Some are short and some are tall.

Things,
Oooh stuff,
Oh objects,
Oooh things,
Oooh general things.

srie
ssre
esree
'sry
:sr'e
ss'reee

Different things are
 all around,
Some on shelves,
some on the ground,
Some are brown,
some things are green,
And every colour inbetween,

Things,
Ooooh structures,
Oh shaaa-apes
Oooh solid matter
Oh things

IDEA FOR RHYMES IN SONGS

GHOST and TOAST (good)

PARK and DARK. (Wicked!)

CARRIER BAG and GARY'S A SLAG
I'm cookin' today!

(stuck on last two verses - need help)

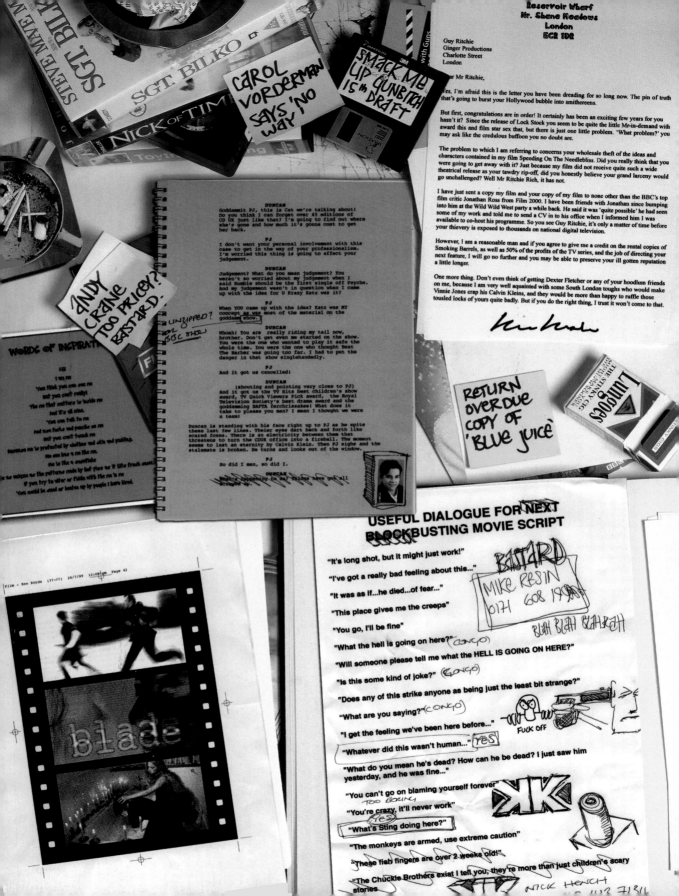

Reservoir Wharf
Nr. Shane Meadows
London
EC2R 1DR

Guy Ritchie
Ginger Productions
Charlotte Street
London

Dear Mr Ritchie,

Yes, I'm afraid this is the letter you have been dreading for so long now. The pin of truth that's going to burst your Hollywood bubble into smithereens.

But first, congratulations are in order! It certainly has been an exciting few years for you hasn't it? Since the release of Lock Stock you seem to be quite the little Mr-in-demand with award this and film star sex that, but there is just one little problem. 'What problem?' you may ask like the credulous buffoon you no doubt are.

The problem to which I am referring concerns your wholesale theft of the ideas and characters contained in my film Speeding On The Needlebliss. Did you really think that you were going to get away with it? Just because my film did not receive quite such a wide theatrical release as your tawdry rip-off, did you honestly believe your grand larceny would go unchallenged? Well Mr Ritchie Rich, it has not.

I have just sent a copy my film and your copy of my film to none other than the BBC's top film critic Jonathan Ross from Film 2000. I have been friends with Jonathan since bumping into him at the Wild Wild West party a while back. He said it was 'quite possible' he had seen some of my work and told me to send a CV in to his office when I informed him I was available to co-host his programme. So you see Guy Ritchie, it's only a matter of time before your thievery is exposed to thousands on national digital television.

However, I am a reasonable man and if you agree to give me a credit on the rental copies of Smoking Barrels, as well as 50% of the profits of the TV series, and the job of directing your next feature, I will go no further and you may be able to preserve your ill gotten reputation a little longer.

One more thing. Don't even think of getting Dexter Fletcher or any of your hoodlum friends on me, because I am very well acquainted with some South London toughs who would make Vinnie Jones crap his Calvin Kleins, and they would be more than happy to ruffle those tousled locks of yours quite badly. But if you do the right thing, I trust it won't come to that.

STEVE MARTIN SGT. BILKO

SGT. BILKO

NICK OF TIME

CAROL VORDERMAN SAYS 'NO WAY'

SMACK ME UP GUNBITCH 15th DRAFT

ANDY CRANE TOO PRICEY? BASTARD.

WORDS OF INSPIRAT...

RETURN OVERDUE COPY OF 'BLUE JUICE'

LUNGOGS STINKY CIG

DUNCAN
Goddammit PJ, this is Cat we're talking about! Do you think I can forget over 45 editions of CD UK just like that? I'm going to find out where she's gone and how much it's gonna cost to get her back.

PJ
I don't want your personal involvement with this case to get in the way of your professionalism. I'm worried this thing is going to affect your judgement.

DUNCAN
Judgement? What do you mean judgement? You weren't so worried about my judgement when I said Rumble should be the first single off Psyche. And my judgement wasn't in question when I came up with the idea for U Krazy Katz was it?

PJ
When YOU came up with the idea? Katz was MY concept as was most of the material on the goddamn show.

is UNZIPPED? *is BBC BTHD*

DUNCAN
Whoah! You are really riding my tail now, brother. Don't get even me started on the show. You were the one who wanted to play it safe the whole time. You were the one who thought Beat The Barber was going too far. I had to put the danger in that show singlehandedly.

And it got us cancelled!

DUNCAN
(shouting and pointing very close to PJ) And it got us the TV Hits best children's show award, TV Quick Viewers Pick award, the Royal Television Society's best drama award and the goddamning BAFTA ferchrissakes! What does it take to please you man? I mean I thought we were a team!

Duncan is standing with his face right up to PJ as he spits these last few lines. Their eyes dart back and forth like scared foxes. There is an electricity between them that threatens to turn the CDUK office into a fireball. The moment seems to last an eternity by Calvin Klein. Then PJ sighs and the stalemate is broken. He turns and looks out of the window.

So did I man, so did I.

DUNCAN
... happening to us? Things have got all screwed up.

Film - Ken Rouda (F2-F7) 26/7/99 12:00pm Page 42

blade

USEFUL DIALOGUE FOR NEXT BLOCKBUSTING MOVIE SCRIPT

"It's long shot, but it might just work!"

"I've got a really bad feeling about this..."

"It was as if...he died...of fear..."

"This place gives me the creeps"

"You go, I'll be fine"

"What the hell is going on here?" (CONGO)

"Will someone please tell me what the HELL IS GOING ON HERE?"

"Is this some kind of joke?" (CONGO)

"Does any of this strike anyone as being just the least bit strange?"

"What are you saying?" (CONGO)

"I get the feeling we've been here before..."

"Whatever did this wasn't human..." YES!

"What do you mean he's dead? How can he be dead? I just saw him yesterday, and he was fine..."

"You can't go on blaming yourself forever" TOO BOUNCY

"You're crazy, it'll never work" YES!

"What's Sting doing here?"

"The monkeys are armed, use extreme caution"

"The fish fingers are over 2 weeks old!"

"These fish fingers are over 2 weeks old! they're more than just children's scary stories..."

"The Chuckle Brothers exist I tell you, they're more than just children's scary stories"

BASTARD
MIKE RESIN
0171 608 1990

BLAH BLAH BLAHBLAH

Fuck off

NICK HENCH

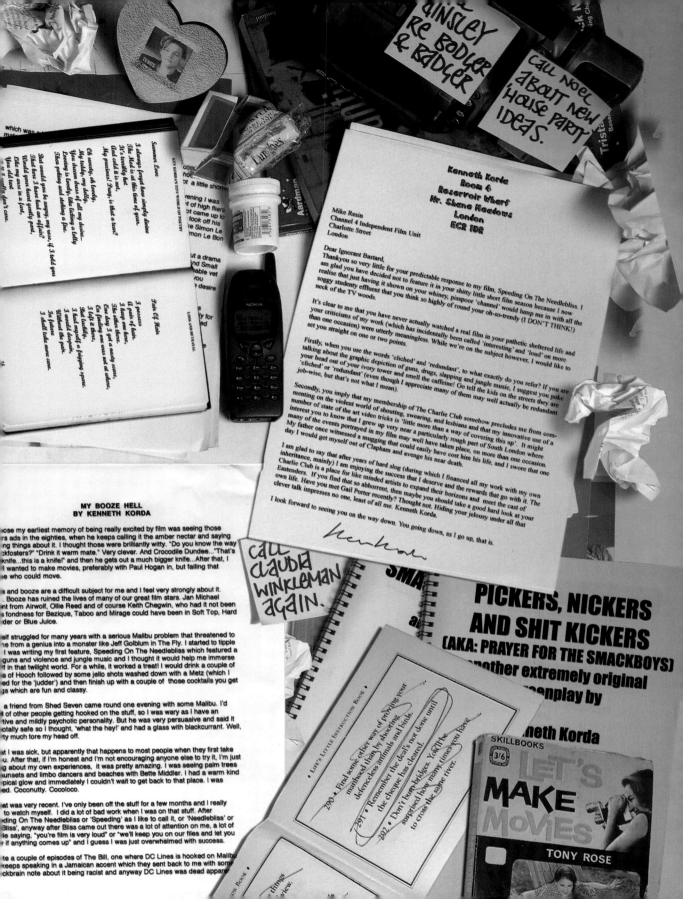

AINSLEY RE BODGER & BADGER

CALL NOEL ABOUT NEW HOUSE PARTY IDEAS.

CALL CLAUDIA WINKLEMAN AGAIN.

Summer Love

I always forget how simply divine
The Med is at this time of year.
It's toasty hot
And cold it is not,
My precious! Pussy, is that a tear?

Oh, swanky, oh lovely,
My darling, my dashing,
You dream doos of all my desire.
Evening is lonely, like tasting a telly
Then pottery and stealing a fine.

But would you be empty, my own, if I told you
That here I have had an affair?
Would you then burst gently apart?
Like my once in a fret,
You old twat
So a softly don't care.

Pain Of Rain

I possess
A pain of rain.
I keep one here,
The other there.
One day I get a rusty score,
See finding one was and at whore,
I left it there.
But luckily,
I think myself a fopping spume.
I would deepish,
Without the pain.
In future
I shall take more care.

Kenneth Korda
Room 4
Reservoir Wharf
Nr. Shane Meadows
London
EC2R 1DR

Mike Resin
Channel 4 Independent Film Unit
Charlotte Street
London

Dear Ignorant Bastard,

Thankyou so very little for your predictable response to my film, Speeding On The Needlebliss. I am glad you have decided not to feature it in your shitty little short film season because I now realise that just having it shown on your whiney, pisspoor 'channel' would lump me in with all the soggy studenty effluent that you think so highly of round your oh-so-trendy (I DON'T THINK!) neck of the TV woods.

It's clear to me that you have never actually watched a real film in your pathetic sheltered life and your criticisms of my work (which has incidentally been called 'interesting' and 'loud' on more than one occasion) were utterly meaningless. While we're on the subject however, I would like to set you straight on one or two points.

Firstly, when you use the words 'cliched' and 'redundant', to what exactly do you refer? If you are talking about the graphic depiction of guns, drugs, slapping and jungle music, I suggest you poke your head out of your ivory tower and smell the caffeine! Go tell the kids on the streets they are 'cliched' or 'redundant' (even though I appreciate many of them may well actually be redundant job-wise, but that's not what I mean).

Secondly, you imply that my membership of The Charlie Club somehow precludes me from commenting on the violent world of shouting, swearing, and lesbians and that my innovative use of a number of state of the art video tricks is 'little more than a way of covering this up'. It might interest you to know that I grew up very near a particularly rough part of South London where many of the events portrayed in my film may well have taken place, on more than one occasion. My father once witnessed a mugging that could easily have cost him his life, and I swore that one day I would get myself out of Clapham and avenge his near death.

I am glad to say that after years of hard slog (during which I financed all my work with my own inheritance, mainly) I am enjoying the success that I deserve and the rewards that go with it. The Charlie Club is a place for like minded artists to expand their horizons and meet the cast of Eastenders. If you find that so abhorrent, then maybe you should take a good hard look at your own life. Have you met Gail Porter recently? Thought not. Hiding your jelousy under all that clever talk impresses no one, least of all me. Kenneth Korda.

I look forward to seeing you on the way down. You going down, as I go up, that is.

MY BOOZE HELL
BY KENNETH KORDA

...ose my earliest memory of being really excited by film was seeing those ...rs ads in the eighties, when he keeps calling it the amber nectar and saying ...g things about it. I thought those were brilliantly witty. "Do you know the way ...ckfosters?" "Drink it warm mate." Very clever. And Crocodile Dundee..."That's ... knife...this is a knife!" and then he gets out a much bigger knife...After that, I ... wanted to make movies, preferably with Paul Hogan in, but failing that ...e who could move.

...s and booze are a difficult subject for me and I feel very strongly about it. ... Booze has ruined the lives of many of our great film stars. Jan Michael ...nt from Airwolf, Ollie Reed and of course Keith Chegwin, who had it not been ...s fondness for Bezique, Taboo and Mirage could have been in Soft Top, Hard ...der or Blue Juice.

...elf struggled for many years with a serious Malibu problem that threatened to ...e from a genius into a monster like Jeff Golblum in The Fly. I started to tipple ... I was writing my first feature, Speeding On The Needlebliss which featured a ... guns and violence and jungle music and I thought it would help me immerse ... in that twilight world. For a while, it worked a treat! I would drink a couple of ...s of Hooch followed by some jello shots washed down with a Metz (which I ...ed for the 'judder') and then finish up with a couple of those cocktails you get ...gs which are fun and classy.

... a friend from Shed Seven came round one evening with some Malibu. I'd ... of other people getting hooked on the stuff, so I was wary as I have an ...tive and mildly psychotic personality. But he was very persuasive and said it ...otally safe so I thought, 'what the hey!' and had a glass with blackcurrant. Well, ...ty much tore my head off.

...t I was sick, but apparently that happens to most people when they first take ...u. After that, if I'm honest and I'm not encouraging anyone else to try it, I'm just ... about my own experiences, it was pretty amazing. I was seeing palm trees ...sunsets and limbo dancers and beaches with Bette Midler. I had a warm kind ...pical glow and immediately I couldn't wait to get back to that place. I was ...ed. Coconutty. Cocoloco.

...t was very recent. I've only been off the stuff for a few months and I really ... watch myself. I did a lot of bad work when I was on that stuff. After ...ding On The Needlebliss or 'Speeding' as I like to call it, or 'Needlebliss' or ...Bliss', anyway after Bliss came out there was a lot of attention on me, a lot of ...le saying, "you're film is very loud" or "we'll keep you on our files and let you ... if anything comes up" and I guess I was just overwhelmed with success.

...te a couple of episodes of The Bill, one where DC Lines is hooked on Malibu ... keeps speaking in a Jamaican accent which they sent back to me with some ...ckbrain note about it being racist and anyway DC Lines was dead appare...

PICKERS, NICKERS AND SHIT KICKERS
(AKA: PRAYER FOR THE SMACKBOYS)
another extremely original screenplay by
Kenneth Korda

Life's Little Instruction Book

290 • Find some other way of proving your manhood than by shooting defenceless animals and birds.

291 • Remember the deal's not done until the cheque has cleared.

292 • Don't burn bridges. You'll be surprised how many times you have to cross the same river.

SKILLBOOKS
3/6
LET'S MAKE MOVIES
TONY ROSE

THE SWEETS OF

The new millennium will be full of exciting changes that will render our lives unrecognisable from the ones we lead today. Transporter beams will move us from A to B quicker than trains or scooters ever could! Man will live in bubbles suspended high above the Earth by string! War will be replaced by a comparison of relative knob sizes! And most excitingly of all, new confectionery will be invented while our old favourites will undergo radical changes of image! Here are few you can expect before the end of the next century.

BROWNBALLS

While these may look like the honeycomb-centred chocballs of old, the truth couldn't be further from, er, that. Brownballs are one of several groundbreaking savoury/sweet hybrids that are set to revolutionise the workplace, the playground and Stroud. Tiny desiccated chicken nuggets are covered in a thin layer of sticky gravy, then freeze-dried. The result is a tasty snack that will ruin your appetite.

MUCKLEY

Ever wished there was a bar that had jammy goo not just inside, but outside too? Until that bar comes along why not try yourself a Muckley! It's got jammy goo outside making it fun to pick up and slippery in hot weather. Inside is a piece of relatively non-toxic* plastifibrelex that is not edible but 60% re-usable (though not recyclable). Just eat or wash off the goo and dip the plastifibrelex into the jam, honey or taramasalata of your choice! It could be simpler, but with Muckley, it isn't!
*Almost certainly carcinogenic.

SCRUNTY NUTPEA FUNCH

No time for a proper lunchtime meal but sick of crisps and cigarettes? Scrunty Nutpea Funch is quite literally, a fun lunch, combining delicious chocolate style paste with frozen peas and lard for a snack that will fill you up with peas, lard and paste. A yummy treat for vegetarians (though Muslims may find the high lard content problematic).

Pick yourself out a nice *BOGIS*

BOGIS

Finally, a bar that combines the two main passions of kiddies everywhere: chocolate and picking your nose! It features delicious minty chocolate with pieces of real bogey (or snot to give it its proper name). The boogers become chewy when the bar is chilled, making it a great way for kids to while away a hot afternoon of violence.

THE FUTURE...

MUNGLERS

As part of The Chocolate Constitution the bar formerly known as Marathon must change its name every ten years to keep customers confused. The name 'Munglers' is the product of over 20 years' exhaustive and costly scientific market research conducted alone in a room by Phil Munglers.

USUKANCHU

From those clever Japanese comes a totally new concept in confectionery design: re-usable sweeties. Taking its inspiration from Opal Fruits and latterly the vastly inferior Starburst, Usukanchu are made of soft, mildly smelly rubber and can also be used as erasers, guaranteeing them a place in every schoolkid's heart and satchel. The fruit flavours run out quickly but if not swallowed the rubber can last up to days longer.

SNATCH

What's in a name? In the case of the Snatch bar, everything! Why? I'll tell you. Snatch is made up of all natural (or 'natch') ingredients, like ground twigs and leaves, making it an ideal way to 'snatch' a healthy bite for dirty minded ('snatch') businessmen on the go. You see?! Snatch! What?

KRAPSTIX

Unlike other dual-finger chocolate-covered wafer treats, Krapstix is made entirely of wafer, but not just any wafer, cheap wafer! Yes, Krapstix is the perfect snack for people who feel guilty about eating sweets because it's mainly air and very low in calories so it won't ruin your appetite or damage your pockets. And if you miss the chocolate, no problem, because from March next year Krapstix will come with an optional sachet of milk chocolate that you can spread yourself. (Estimated sachet price £2.46)

HENK

Here's a new look for an old favourite with a few changes that will appeal to value conscious consumers and taste fans alike! Henk does away with sickly caramel and chocolate in favour of a hard cocoa based resin that can be gnawed or licked over a period of weeks. It also features bits of real orange peel. Yes.

THE TOY PATIENT

At last kids can enjoy the tedious historical romance of *The English Patient*, with our special new stuffed-toy read-along adaptation – guaranteed to not meet National Shiteracy Guidelines!

Nurse Hana is looking after a patient. He is very badly burnt all over.
"What's your name?" asks Nurse Hana.
"I don't know, I can't remember" he replies.
"Can I call you Burnie?" she asks.
"Wait!" says the patient, "I think I'm going to have a multi-award-winning, three hour flashback!"

New Words: Flashback, Multi-award-winnin[g]

The patient is having a flashback. He, Katherine and Geoffrey have found some ancient cave paintings.
"What do they mean?" asks Katherine.
"They signify that man evolved from the sea, a place without boundaries or ownership" explains the patient.
"I don't understand," says Geoffrey.

"They mean I'm going to have sex with your wife."

New words: Ownership, Sex,   Wife

Katherine is showing her drawings to the patient.
"Would you like to stick my pictures in your book?" she asks.
"I beg your pardon?" says the patient.
"Would you like to stick your pictures up my book?" says Katherine.
"I'm sorry, I don't understand" says the patient.

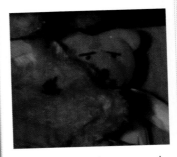

"Oh, shut up, shag me and kill me you gorgeous bastard!" says Katherine.

New Words: Gorgeous, Shag,   Kill

Katherine and the patient are having a bath.
"Tell me, what do you love?" asks the patient.
"Hedgehogs, Harpers and Queen, High Street Ken on a Saturday," replies Katherine. "What about you?"
"Beer, fags, football, one-night stands with no strings attached," answers the patient.

New Words: Harpers & Queen, Beer, Fags

Geoffrey has tried to kill the patient with his plane, but he has missed.
"Geoffrey's dead!" says the patient. "Excellent!"
Poor Katherine is terribly injured.
"What are you doing here?" asks the patient.
"Oh, desperate plot device darling," she replies.

New Words: Desperate, Plot,   Device

The patient has taken Katherine back to the cave.
"I love you," she whispers.
"Yes, yes, I love you too," answers the patient.
"Promise you'll never leave me?" she asks.
"I promise. I'll never leave you," he replies.
"Kiss me," she says, and they kiss.
"Right then, I'm off," says the patient. "Bye!"

New Words: Love, Kiss, I'm Off,   Bye

The flashback has finished. Suddenly Katherine returns.
"I'm not dead, I ran out of batteries. Now you have to stay with me forever!" she says.
"Mon dieu! She's the Duracell Bunny!" exclaims Nurse Hana.
Then, all of a sudden, an Oscar arrives.
"This is tragic!" he says, "I love it! Have six of me!"

New Words: Oscar, Tragic

VINYL JUSTICE DEPARTMENT:
GUIDELINES FOR COMPILATION TAPES

The compiling of tracks onto a cassette for a friend or your own personal use is an essential part of listening to music on a regular basis. If the compilation is for you then it serves to create an uninterrupted hits session that does away with the irksome skipping or fast forwarding of crap tracks necessary with many albums. If the 'compi' is for a friend it's the perfect way to dazzle them with your obscure music knowledge and indeed, to increase the likelihood of them having something decent to listen to when you go round to their place for an evening. But there are certain basic guidelines which should be adhered for the creation of a truly classic compi.

KEEP A CONSISTENT MOOD

It takes a highly skilled compi-maker to follow Anarchy In The UK by The Sex Pistols with We Are Detective by the Thompson Twins successfully. It can be done, but if the whole compilation is not just right you run the risk of creating an unlistenable nightmare that will please no-one. A safer option for the novice is deciding on the mood you want to achieve before starting. Here are a few popular choices:

1. Mellow.

These are compis to listen to late at night when everyone is wrecked and has lost the power of speech. They could feature a few ballads from the likes of Neil Young, David Bowie, Lou Reed or Van Morrison, or some ambient noodling from Brian Eno, Stereolab, The High Llamas or Aphex Twin. It's entirely up to you. Just be careful not to suddenly stick AC/DC on to fill the end of a side.

2. New Love

This is the compi you make for your new girl/boyfriend, packed with beautiful tunes that you think express the profound feelings you're too scared to articulate. No Radiohead then. Unless you expect the relationship to end fairly soon.

3. Non Stop House/Techno Mix

The ideal opportunity to show off those phenomenal mixing skills, at least to yourself, because no-one you give this compi to is ever going to be bothered to listen to it right the way through, unless they're on extremely hard drugs, in which case they will have to go to prison. Gottit?

4. Obscuro Indy Weirdfest

To be truly effective this compi should not contain a single popular or recognisable track and should be recorded entirely from deleted or bootleg vinyl, preferably very scratched.

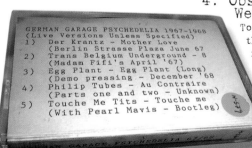

Bands that you never knew existed and bands that never deserved to exist all jostle for obscurity on one C90 testament to your all conquering intimacy with music that no-one wants to listen to.

AVOID THE EPICS AND THE NOVELTIES

Songs like Bohemian Rhapsody, Light My Fire and almost anything by the Beta Band or Can that go on for over seven minutes may be impressive and

epic when you first hear them, but after the twentieth time, you'll regret they ever made it to the compi. Keep it short and sweet if you want to keep the listener interested. By the same token, songs that on first listen are amusingly weird or 'zany' will almost certainly grate after only three or four plays. "Oh God," the listener will think, "it's that Ween / They Might be Giants / Bis track again," and you'll lose them.

SPACE OUT THE ARTISTS

If you are including one or more songs from a single album or artist, the tracks should be spaced out to give the illusion of greater variety and depth of musical knowledge.

FILL THE WHOLE TAPE

It is an offence to make a compi that stops suddenly on side two and has to be fast forwarded to start again. It is also unacceptable to pad the second half of the tape with

the rest of the album you last used. If you do not have enough material for the full 60 or 90 minute compi (45 minutes is an insult) then you should either wait until you do, or collect some imaginative 'filler material' that can pad it out. This could be anything from very short stupid songs and jingles, to comedy and bits of dialogue from your favourite films and TV programmes (although using the bits of dialogue on the Pulp Fiction and Reservoir Dogs soundtracks is a serious offence punishable by punching). You should never allow a song to be cut off half way through at the end of a side. That's what filler material is there for.

PAY ATTENTION TO INLAY DESIGN

Once your compi is finished, it's time to think about the cover art. Just scrawling the tracks on the inlay provided or worse, not including track details at all, will betray a lack of true compi dedication. You can start by using different coloured pens and silver markers on the tape then work your way to drawing on the cover and pasting together images that you feel express the content therein. Remember, a great looking compi stands less chance of being played just once then languishing on the dashboard of someone's car until it warps in the sun. Although that isn't true, it's a comforting thought.

no inlay, indication of content, no attention to design, artists probably bunched together with gaps at the end of each side. A disgrace.

Now you're ready to make your own classic compi. But remember, if you deviate from these guidelines in any way whatsoever, there will be absolutely no consequences. And no, following Beck with Jimmy The Hoover is not eclectic, it's just stupid and naughty.

SUCCESSFUL STREET SPITTING

There's no better way to impress friends and strangers alike than a stylish spit. Spitting has become a modern street art, capable of expressing an individual's personality and temperament with unparalleled style and immediacy.

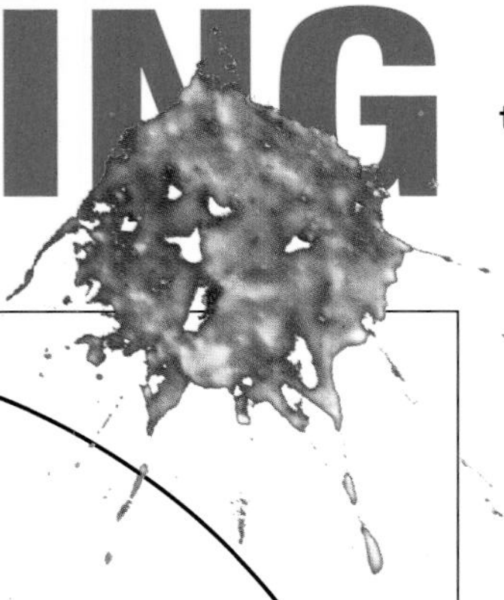

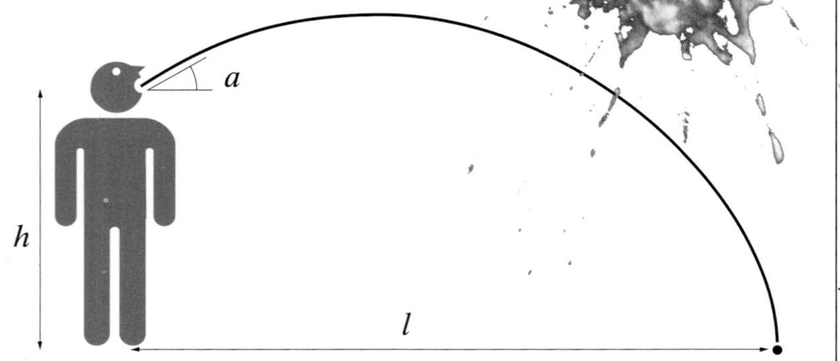

of all spits, the spray is easy to perform but hard to perfect. The aim is to randomly spray watery spit from between the teeth in as wide a circumference as possible. To the casual observer it might seem as if the spit has gone terribly wrong, so broad and random is its range. But the trained eye knows full well that this powerful method, when successfully executed, can target up to five passers-by with deadly accuracy, whilst appearing to be accidental.

Fig 1. A projectile flob of mass m expelled with a force f from a head angled at a degrees from a height h will reach a distance l where
$$l = f\,(m^{-2})g^2 \tan a\ h^{-1}$$

The Projectile Flob

This entry-level spit was brought to popular attention by Leonardo di Caprio and Kate Winslet in the film 'Titanic'. The simple aim is to shoot a ball of snot as fast and far from the mouth as possible. First conjure as much heavy gelatinous mucus from the back of the throat as possible, and roll it into a firm ball with the tongue. Manoeuvre the ball into position between the lips, making sure your teeth are parted wide enough to let the projectile pass. Now take a deep breath (taking care not to suck the snot back down your throat) and blow as hard and fast as possible.

The Dribble

The Dribble, perhaps the most skilled of all spits, can only be executed while motionless. The aim is to let a thin white string of foamy, snotty spit extend like a plumb-line from the mouth until it reaches the ground. The slower the strand's progression downwards, the better. The dribble is best performed with a gang of mates loitering outside a newsagent, or on public transport when people are watching. When properly performed, the dribble can be highly intimidating and impressive.

The Spray

Considered the most anti-social

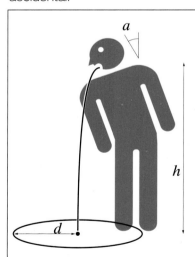

Fig 2. A dribble of volume v expelled from a head angled at a degrees from a height h will produce a splat of diameter d where
$$d = 4/3\ (v^{-3})g^2 \cos a\ h^{-1}$$

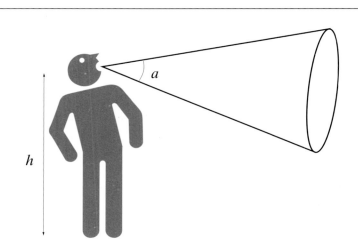

Fig 3. A spray of volume v expelled with a force f from a height h will spatter any object within a cone of apex angle a where $a = 4/3\ (v^{-3})g^2 \cos f\ h^{-1}$

The Hawk

A difficult spit that is easy to perform accidentally, but difficult to execute on request. The desired effect is to be clearing the throat with loud guttural hawking sounds, when suddenly a small unpredicted fleck of throat glue shoots out directly from the base of the windpipe, through the mouth and out into the world. Note that there is no use of tongue here and little visible preparation. This is another excellent way to spit on or at someone 'accidentally'. Just be sure to laugh, apologise and act surprised.

The Diseased Flob

This is a spit that the amateur will only be capable of producing once or twice annually, but that the professional must be able to call upon all year round. The key here is in the tortured coughing it takes to bring the diseased phlegm up from the lungs to the mouth. To qualify, the phlegm must be half in the lungs and half hanging from the mouth for as long as possible, like oral ectoplasm. Many of the world's best diseased spitters can be seen gathered around benches outside main line railway stations clasping bottles of Old English Cider and smoking B&H, exchanging notes on technique and style.

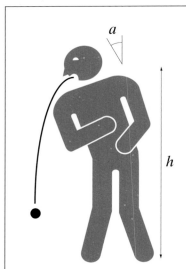

Fig 4. A diseased flob of mass m expelled with a force f from a head angled at a degrees from a height h has a probability p of containing lung matter where
$$p = f\ (m^{-2})g^2 \tan a\ h^{-1}$$

BOLLOCKBUSTERS

FREE cut-out-and-keep

ROBOT MOVIE MARATHON

by KENNETH KORDA

Short Circuit Two/ 1986

Johnny Five is the star of this movie. It is a more realistic look into robotics than other humanoid-driven films and based on existing science. Watch out for the naive yet hilarious inventor who is an Indian man like in *It Ain't Half Hot Mum* which is good but Windsor Davies is a shit robot. SHIT.

Project Shadowchaser/ 1992

If I'm honest I'd have to say I haven't seen this one, but I know the video box very well from my afternoons of hesitation in Bollockbusters. Blonde muscly cyborg man, guns. That is a proven formula.

Making Mr Right/ 1976

Featuring the very funny Mr John Malkovich as an uptight scientist who creates a porn crazed robot in his own image. His wife likes the robot better than him or something. Dirty and stupid but not that good when I think about it.

Demon Seed/ 1980, 1978

I do not generally approve of robots forcibly impregnating ladies, but this filthy yet fun movie features a good deal of important philosophy as well as a huge one of those floppy pyramid puzzles that became popular after people grew tired of Rubik's cubes. This was later remade as *Princess Caraboo*. I'm going now. Bye!

PORKY' O'ROURKE'S
'INTO THE MIND OF THE SERIAL KILLER'

Yes. My name is Porky O'Rourke. I played Brad Pigg in the terrifying thriller, 'Seven Dwarves'. My character was a hard-snouted but impulsive detective on the trail of an insane psychopathic killer. As preparation for the role I watched some other films about serial killers and thought about them for a while on the tube and the lavvy. As a result I'm something of an expert on the habits and motivations of these remarkable people. So join me now as we journey... into the mind of the serial killer! Have I said that already?

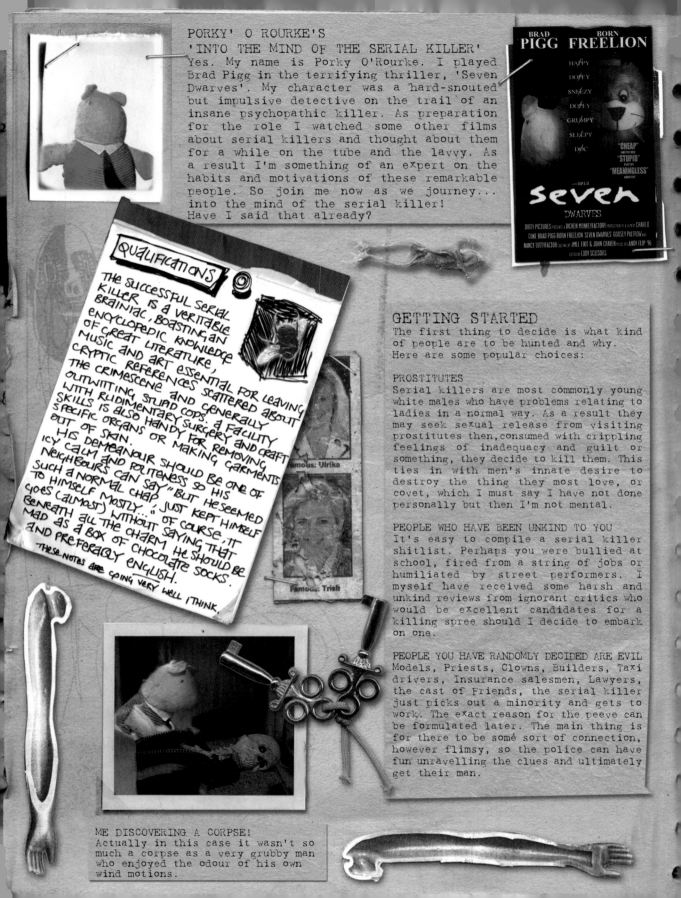

BRAD **PIGG** BORN **FREELION**

HAPPY
DOPEY
SNEEZY
DOPEY
GRUMPY
SLEEPY
DOC

"CHEAP" *UNRESTRICTED*
"STUPID" *PLAYBOY*
"MEANINGLESS" *VARIETY*

seven
DWARVES

DIRTY PICTURES PRESENTS A DICKEN MONKEYFACTORY PRODUCTION A FILM BY CHARLIE COKE BRAD PIGG BORN FREELION SEVEN DWARVES GOOSEY PALTROW AND NANCY LUTTYFACTOR EDITING BY JIMLE FIXIT & JOHN CRAVEN MUSIC BY SANDY FLIP '96 EDITED BY EDDY SCISSORS

QUALIFICATIONS

The successful serial killer is a veritable BRAINIAC, boasting an encyclopedic knowledge of great literature, music and art essential for leaving cryptic references scattered about the crimescene and generally outwitting stupid cops. A facility with rudimentary surgery and craft skills is also handy for removing specific organs or making garments out of skin.

His demeanour should be one of icy calm and politeness so his neighbours can say "But he seemed such a normal chap, just kept himself to himself mostly..." of course, it goes (almost) without saying that mad as a box of chocolate socks. Beneath all the charm he should be and preferably English.

THESE NOTES ARE GOING VERY WELL I THINK.

Famous: Ulrika

Famous: Trish

ME DISCOVERING A CORPSE!
Actually in this case it wasn't so much a corpse as a very grubby man who enjoyed the odour of his own wind motions.

GETTING STARTED

The first thing to decide is what kind of people are to be hunted and why. Here are some popular choices:

PROSTITUTES
Serial killers are most commonly young white males who have problems relating to ladies in a normal way. As a result they may seek sexual release from visiting prostitutes then, consumed with crippling feelings of inadequacy and guilt or something, they decide to kill them. This ties in with men's innate desire to destroy the thing they most love, or covet, which I must say I have not done personally but then I'm not mental.

PEOPLE WHO HAVE BEEN UNKIND TO YOU
It's easy to compile a serial killer shitlist. Perhaps you were bullied at school, fired from a string of jobs or humiliated by street performers. I myself have received some harsh and unkind reviews from ignorant critics who would be excellent candidates for a killing spree should I decide to embark on one.

PEOPLE YOU HAVE RANDOMLY DECIDED ARE EVIL
Models, Priests, Clowns, Builders, Taxi drivers, Insurance salesmen, Lawyers, the cast of Friends, the serial killer just picks out a minority and gets to work. The exact reason for the peeve can be formulated later. The main thing is for there to be some sort of connection, however flimsy, so the police can have fun unravelling the clues and ultimately get their man.

MODUS OPERANDI (They way they do it)

Once the victims have been selected, the serial killer must decide on what method he will employ to indulge his madness. The amateur nutcake will be content with stabbing, strangling, shooting and maybe a bit of dismembering, but for the professional it's, quite literally, all in the execution!

Every murder should be like a work of modern art, with methods carefully chosen to say something special about the victim. Killing a politician? Tie him up in red tape and drown him in bullshit. Or a tabloid reporter? stuff their copy down their throats and tattoo headlines all over their body with acid, that'll teach 'em! It is imperative to develop a style distinctive enough to lead the coppers straight to the perpetrator's loony lair (or nutty room). And there should always be some kind of 'calling card', like beetles in the nostril, or marbles up the arse, you know the kind of thing, it's like a signature on the canvas.

HED-EX - SPECIAL DELIVERY! The old
'wife's-head-in-the-box' routine!

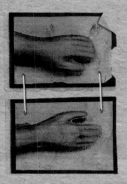

NUTTY ROOM

If you imagine the scene of the crime as the serial killer's exhibition space, then the nutty room is their studio and a wonderful opportunity for demonstrating the depth and complexity of their loonosity (or loonism). Ideally located beneath a perfectly normal looking house, the room generally falls into one of these two categories:

CHILLINGLY SPARTAN

Neon lit and clinically clean, this room is an indication of the extent to which the killer's murderous torment has been internalised (what?). Medical equipment and cleaning products are carefully arranged on stainless steel worktops and textbooks are stacked in alphabetical order on shelves. It seems to be the work of a compulsively ordered mind, but as we know, that couldn't be further from the truth! It's an insane mess of a mind! Insane I tell you! Not ordered at all! ...I over-egged the pudding there, didn't I?

DARK AND GRIM

Lit by a bare 40-watt bulb and resplendent in disgustitude, this is the nutty room paradigm. Insects scuttle and buzz about the dust and filth. Photographs of victims are pinned to walls adorned with crazy scribbles while unspecified organs and limbs sit pickling in yellowed jars. (Can you see all this? I think I'm really describing the tits off it, don't you?) Notebooks lie open, stuffed with tiny demented scrawls and crudely affixed pictures of Hitler and such. NOT Henry Kelly. And to round it all off nicely, a foul stench should pervade, sending the cops retching and reaching for their hankies.

WELL MY FRIENDS, THAT'S ABOUT ALL YOU NEED TO KNOW ABOUT THE TWISTED WORLD OF THE SERIAL KILLER. OF COURSE MURDER IS A TERRIBLE BUSINESS, NO MATTER HOW COOL AND INTERESTING IT MAY SEEM, BUT WE SHOULDN'T FORGET THAT IT ALSO CONTINUES TO INSPIRE MANY FUN, HIGH QUALITY MOVIES PROVIDING MUCH NEEDED INCOME FOR TALENTED ACTORS LIKE ME

Porky O Rourke

This corner soaked in cyanide in case of emergency

Max. 100 ~~years~~

ADAM AND JOE
EXAMINATION ~~BOARD~~ RED
General Certificate Examination

ENGLISH LITERATURE
Tuesday 6th June 1999. 2 hours *of hell*

Answer all the questions
or we will destroy your life
You should pay careful attention to spelling, punctuation, and handwriting.

Section A

Read the following extract from Shakesbeare's 'Romeo and Juliette Bravo' carefully and answer the questions which follow it.

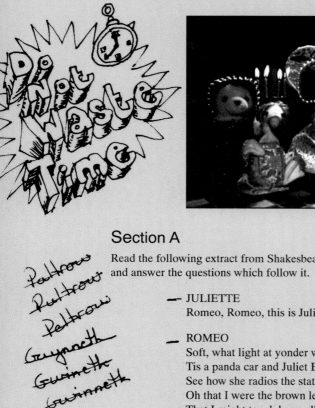

— JULIETTE
Romeo, Romeo, this is Juliet Bravo; wherefore art thou, over?   (2)

— ROMEO
Soft, what light at yonder window breaks?
Tis a panda car and Juliet Bravo is within!
See how she radios the station.
Oh that I were the brown leather glove on her hand,
That I might touch her walkie-talkie!   (7)

— JULIETTE
Oh, I'm horny; horny, horny horny.
So horny; horny, horny, horny.   (9)

— ROMEO
How sweet soft and sensuous to stroke
Are the feathers on thine arse,
Thus from my lips doth my tongue protrude
And shoveth down thine beak
As to snog thine face right off.   (14)

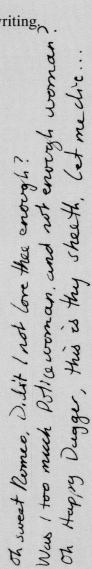

Oh sweet Romeo, D.Lit I not love thee enough?
Was I too much P.O.liceman, and not enough woman?
Oh Happy Dagger, this is thy sheath, let me die....

A B C D E F ?? I, J, K, L, M, N, O, P, Q, ?, ?, T, U, V, W, X, Y,

Hello, I'm Shakespeare, please will you Help alleviate the suffering of millions of young people around the world by travelling back in time and killing me. Thankyou

1.Describe in your own words the reasons why stern female police officers are particularly sexually attractive. Do not use more than 10, 0000 words. (20 marks)

2.Under (a), (b) and (c) write down three filthy meanings which you think the phrase 'walkie-talkie' (line 7) might have in this context. Also draw pictures. *EASY !* (10 marks)

3. Describe in someone elses's words what kind of sonnets Shakesbeare might have written
   if he had copped off with the following;

King Leer ← (a) Samantha Janus → *Love's Labours Lost*
(b) Anne Heche → *Play Your Cards Right*
Turn of the screw?? ← (c) Jenny Powell → *Play Your Cards Right*
(d) Handy Andy from 'Changing Rooms'

– Patronising
– Handcuffs
– Clean
– Probably single (10 marks)

4.Describe in a made-up alien language why Shakesbeare's repeated use of the word 'horny' is particularly effective (line 8). Also describe how this couplet might be turned into a dancefloor smash, what chart position it might reach, what words Dr. Fox might use to introduce it on the Pepsi Chart Rundown, and why. (10 marks)

Section B

Write about 100-150 words on **one** of the following;

Either (a) Why theatre seats are so tiny, stage actors shout all the time, most plays are boring and they only ever sell tiny tubs of ice cream and Maltesers.

Or (b)Why Dame Judi Dench is the supposedly the greatest actress in the history of the known universe when all she's been in on telly are a thousand crappy sitcoms.

Or (c)If Shakesbeare were alive today, would he write for Neighbours or Home and Away? In what way would the amount of clothing worn by performers in each contribute to his choice?

Or (d)"All plays are improved when the cast are on roller skates" – discuss. (50 marks)

Fiennes. Fynnes Fiens Fines

Goodnight sweet sleeping policewoman, Thine tireless fight against crime was matched only By thine struggle with the male dominated heirarchy Within the police force itself. Thus, with a kiss, I die

GUIDE TO EXAM CHEATOLOGY

Exams are one of man's greatest miseries, guaranteed to cloud the best summers of your life with dark doom. For those of us who find it hard to concentrate on intensely boring subjects, or find it impossible to revise when the sun's out or there's something good on telly, the only way to avoid total disaster is to cheat. Although it's silly and dangerous, cheating can also be very exciting and improve your grades significantly. If you choose to do it, the only thing you'll need to study is our guide to classic exam cheatology.

COPYING YOUR NEIGHBOUR'S PAPER

You've cultivated this manoeuvre throughout your education. You've perfected the art of looking to your extreme left or right without moving your head, of casually resting your head against your hand in order to shield your wandering eyes, and of dropping a pen and letting it roll towards a clever classmates desk so you can have a peek on your way to fetch it. But be warned. When you enter the exam hall on that fateful day, you will find yourself sat at least two metres from your neighbour. All your hard learnt skills will be rendered useless.

WRITING CRIB NOTES ON YOUR BODY

Attempting this is a bad idea. In the heat of exam halls, sweat will cause your notes to smear illegibly or soak through your shirt, exposing your crime. When caught by a very stupid teacher, you can try saying that you're so keen on the subject that you get a specially themed tattoo. When that fails, you're busted.

CHEAT SHEETS

A good cheat sheet is an exercise in miniaturization. The smaller the sheet, the less likely it is to be found, and the faster you can eat it in an emergency. The smaller the writing on your sheet, the more contraband information you can squeeze onto it. The best pen to use is a professional Rotring. With tiny nibs officially designed for artists and draughtsmen, everyone knows they're really designed for writing the tiniest cheat sheets humanly possible. And if you fail your exams, at least you can scrape a living engraving people's names on grains of rice.

POINTY PINKY

HIDING YOUR CHEAT SHEET

Now that you've written your cheat sheet, you have to decide where to hide it. Consider these tried and tested ideas...

a) In your pencil case: a common but risky technique. The best pencil case to use is a tin maths equipment box with a flip-top lid. If you use an inkpen, simply hide your sheet under a piece of blotting paper. Make regular use of your set square and ruler and take a peek at your cheat sheet each time.

b) In your pants: an ideal contemporary hiding place. Teachers are no longer allowed anywhere near their pupil's pants, especially under exam conditions. Regular pant adjustment is a natural human activity, particularly under sweaty exam conditions, and also serves as an ideal cover for cheat-sheet reference. If they bust you, scream rape.

In the toilet cistern: this time-worn classic is risky because it's so well-known. First work out which toilets are nearest the exam hall. Seal your cheat sheet in a plastic bag & plant it in the cistern. Frequent bowel movements will not seem out of place in the high-pressure atmosphere of the exam, and teachers are no longer allowed to watch while their pupils go to the toilet.

d) In Plain Sight: this is our recommended technique. First, acquire some exam-style lined paper, either from an earlier exam or from a friend. Now write your cheat notes on it in normal-sized writing as if it is your actual exam answer paper. Put the appropriate headings at the top of the page, and number your notes as you would do your real answers. Conceal this in a pile of blank sheets. Now all you have to do is get inside the exam hall, get to your desk, and place your stack of 'blank' paper on top of the stack that's already been laid out for you. After twenty minutes or so, you can openly display it on your desk for reference. Teachers will admire your disciplined approach to exam technique, and you'll be in cheat heaven

A&J 37

KEN KORDA'S HISTORY OF THE MOVIES

PART ONE
THE BIRTH OF CINEMA

Hello, I'm Ken Korda! Welcome to my history of the mooovies. The origins of the cinema can be traced back more than thirty-five thousand years to the first known prehistoric feature films, such as 'Clan of the Cave Bear' starring Daryl Hannah. Scholars believe that 'Cave Bear' was photographed through a sheep's skull directly onto moist bulrushes, which were then developed in a bowl of lemon juice and urine and edited with a flinty stone.

Early Neolithic projectors were also apparently nothing more than a boar's skull with a powerful candle inside. Once developed, the aforementioned moist bulrushes would be wound around twigs and pulled at speed through the skull, causing a bright photo-realistic moving image to shoot from the nostrils onto the cave walls, as well as hi-fi quality stereo sound.

Prehistoric audiences huddled in awe before such movies as 'Quest for Fire' with Rae Dawn Chong and 'Caveman' with Ringo Starr. Though the camerawork was primitive and the dialogue little more than grunts and moans, extensive nudity helped make these early films extremely popular. Man had fallen in love with the movies.

PART TWO
THE GOLDEN AGE OF COMEDY

The first ever comedy film was of course 'The Flintstones' starring cuddly John Goodman and made in stone-age times. Not only is this film laugh-out-loud funny from start to finish, but it's a valuable resource for historians and scholars. It's the only film to capture an authentic living Neolithic town in full living detail, and includes some of the earliest filmed evidence of mankind using friendly dinosaurs for transport.

Despite the awesome chuckle power of Goodman and co, film audiences' tastes were evolving rapidly. By the turn of the century many had discovered clothes and houses and cars, and began to demand less sophisticated lightweight family entertainment. The next significant period in the evolution of film comedy is marked by the arrival of the 'Canine Cop' period. 'Turner and Hooch', made in 1808, starred the world's greatest living actor Tom Hanks as a cop who teams up with a crime-solving dog, with hilariously thrilling results. 'K-9', made in 1809, starred the world's second greatest living actor, James Belushi, as a cop who teams up with a slightly smaller crime-solving dog, with almost exactly equally hilariously thrilling results.

The enormous popularity of these 'Canine Cop' movies paved the way for many of the world's best loved old comedies. Top teams like Smith & Jones, Cannon & Ball and the cast of 'Are You Being Served' were given the opportunity to create big screen masterworks like 'Morons from Outer Space' (1820), 'The Boys in Blue' (1821) and 'Are You Being Served The Movie' (yes we are, and we're loving it!!!) (also 1812).

In those days many comedy films were shot at high speed, making everything in them much funnier. The modern digitally restored versions of these films are slowed down to normal pace, but the full original glory can be easily retrieved by watching them in fast forward. Of course no discussion of the history of comedy films would be complete without a mention of 'The Full Monty' and 'Bean', two films which may well have pushed the concept of laughter and comedy as far as it can go. It may finally be time for comedy to hang up its hat and make way for something new.

PART THREE
THE GREAT HORROR FILMS

Throughout history, great horror movies have taught us that there are few things more horrifying than terror and that nothing is quite as terrifying as being truly horrified. It's also true to say the frightening can often be very very scary indeed. The earliest horror films scare us more through gratuitous gore than subtle suggestion, and that's the way uh-huh, ooh-hoo, I like it.

Classic old horror films include 'Amityville Four – The Wendyhouse' (1850) starring Katie Hill and Macaulay Culkin, 'Pet Cemetery Two – Electric Boogaloo' (1864) starring Clive Dunn, and 'The Boogens' (1894) starring little Gary Coleman. All these films explore the idea that frightening things often jump out at you when you're least expecting them. This theme is further explored in films like 'C.H.U.D.' starring a young Martin Clunes as the leader of a group of mutated underground sewer dwellers, and 'The Ghoulies' starring the young Matthew Kelly as a small boy involved in acting in a bad horror film.

But it wasn't until the eighteen seventies, when censorship finally ended and Video Nasties were introduced by the government, that horror films came into their brutally violent own. Now there was no limit to the disgusting carnage that filmmakers could put on screen, and no limit to the amount of time film fans could spend frame-advancing the best bits.

Recommended Video Nasties include any film whose title begins with the word 'Don't', because you know they will, and that they'll be punished for it!

PART FOUR
THE ADULT FILM INDUSTRY

When discussing the evolution of the adult entertainment industry, one film towers above all others. It is of course 'The Lover' (1543) starring Jane Marsh and an extremely lucky bastard, a young Chinese gentleman with no professional acting experience whatsoever. Possibly the most thrillingly erotic work of cinema ever produced, 'The Lover' is a complex and difficult film that rewards repeat viewings and is widely available in mainstream video stores for less than a tenner without having to go into an actual sex shop.

Marsh (also known as The Sinner from Pinner, which would have made a better title in my opinion) plays young Sally McGoo, a bored, randy schoolgirl in a tiny dress, trapped alone in a very hot sweaty country. One moment she's on her way to school on a ferry, the next moment she's been whisked off in a Rolls Royce by the aforementioned lucky bastard young Chinese gentleman. Seconds later (you don't even need to fast forward, unless you're in a hurry) they arrive at his dirty love lair where he teaches her the art of oriental floor polishing.

When I say oriental floor polishing I am not employing cheap innuendo. The scene in question is a key moment in the evolution of cinematic love making. Young Miss McGoo is being ravished by the oriental gentleman in such a way that he pushes her right across the floor from one corner to another, without the use of his hands or feet, or hers for that matter. He just uses his cock, you see. A truly bravura moment which possesses so much sensual power that I have never been able to watch beyond it. Other recommended classics of erotic cinema include 'The Lover's Guide' parts one and two (1908), 'The Porkies Trilogy' 1923-28), and seasons one-to-fifteen of 'Countdown' with Carol Vorderman. I'm going now, bye!

BOLLOCKBUSTERS

YOURS TO THROW AWAY THIS WEEK AT BOLLOCKBUSTERS, WITH EVERY RENTAL OF CADDYSHACK 2!

TOYTRAINSPOTTING

At last, this classic tale of sherbert addiction is available in its fully restored two-minute director's cut version. A film which manages to be both a chilling warning about the dangers of drugs and a thrilling advert for how great they are. Rent this title more than three hundred times and receive a limited edition syringe/strap set and commemorative anal suppositories. And remember, new laws state that anyone who hasn't seen this film by the year 2005 will automatically have ten years added to their age.

SHAKESBEARE IN LOVE

It won so many awards it has to be good! And yet, when you sit down and watch it, you realise that it's just a load of stuffed toys. This special BOLLOCK-BUSTERS edition features Goosey Paltrow's tearful speech at the Oscars, as well as sixty hours of out-takes, deleted scenes and adverts you've seen a million times on the telly. If you're wet and quite boring you'll love this film. Also features Ralph Fiennes' brother's bear arse! And Goosey Paltrow's nips. Limply superb!

ALLY McSQUEAL

Hooray! Now the legal profession's whiniest mouse is available to watch over and over in the relative comfort of your squat. Marvel at the devastating writing skill with which relations between male and female are laid bare by Michelle Pfeiffer's husband. We love it when they come out with those bitchy one-liners and break into those impromptu song and dance routines, don't we? Of course we do, because we are as lonely and pathetic as Ally herself!

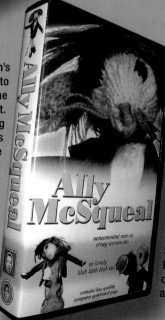

STUFFED TREK: THE TOY GENERATION

If you've seen absolutely every new film that's come out in the last 20 years, then it's probably time for *Extreme Measures* with Hugh Grant. If you're thinking, 'but that was quite good' then it's time to start renting things that are being repeated every two weeks on TV because they contain moving and talking that you may not have seen before. If so, then what could be better than this? A brand new episode of Stuffed Trek featuring Jean Pork Pighard, Woof, Datoy, and of course the terrifying tennis playing alien race...The Bjorn Borg!

OFFER SUBJECT TO USUAL BOLLOCKBUSTER RENTAL STIPULATIONS

1. All films must be rented along with several emergency back-ups in case your mates complain about your choice.
2. All films must be left in your front room unwatched until they are several days overdue, so you can pay an insultingly high fine when you finally get it together to take the frigging things back, by which time you could have actually just bought copies of all of them at Tower.
3. Should you bring back a faulty film, Bollockbusters reserves the right to check it in one of our super-correcto-image-restoring video players so it looks absolutely fine, then tell you it's your tracking and charge you extra. Our staff will be happy to argue for hours about this.
4. In the event that you get a film home only to find that our staff have put the wrong tape inside and instead of this week's biggest rental smash you have a copy of *Nuns On The Run*, Bollockbusters have the right to say it's your fault and refuse to exchange the tape.
5. If you have any questions about Bollockbuster policy please take them up with our staff who will be more than happy to ignore you for a very long time while they talk on the phone to their mate Keith about how wicked *Wild Wild West* was.

BOLLOCKBUSTERS
MEMBERSHIT CARD

TOYTANIC

THE SMALL SCREENPLAY: PART 1

For your reading pleasure: the original script of the most tragic movie ever made!

1. INT: OLD ROSE'S HOUSE – DAY

Old raggedy toy pig ROSE is on the phone the YELLOW PAGES on her lap.

OLD ROSE: Hello, I don't suppose you you've got 'Fly Fishing' by JR Hartley? Oh you do! Wonderful! And I don't suppose you could find the priceless medallion I lost when Toytanic sank eighty-six years ago? You can! Marvellous, I'll be right over!

2. INT: SALVAGE SHIP LAB AREA – DAY

CLOSE on a Charcoal drawing of a young posed pig, nude but for a large square pendant around her neck. OLD ROSE and the SALVAGE CREW stare at it glassy eyed, on account of the fact that their eyes are made of glass.

OLD ROSE: There it is. My precious medallion. It was given to me as an engagement present. I was wearing it when we went down.

ANATOY: Yes, but were you wearing it when the ship sank?

BODINE: Will you help us find it Rose? Are you ready to go back to Toytanic?

OLD ROSE: Yes. But first I'm going to tell you a very long, stupid story about something that never happened. Toytanic was called the ship of dreams. But to me, it was the ship of shit. . .

3. EXT: SOUTHAMPTON DOCK – DAY

Crap synthesised MUSIC starts; choral singing signifying awe. Crowds of excited toys swarm around the vast hulk of the TOYTANIC. A posh CAR pulls up and out steps YOUNG ROSE, her piggy mother RUTH and her brutish Action Man fiancé CAL.

ROSE: (pompous) Ugh, it's pathetic!

CAL: You can be blasé about some things Rose my darling, but not Toytanic.

ROSE: It looks like it's made out of cardboard, bendy straws and string!

CAL: The highest quality bendy straws known to man my dear, and no less than three layers of perfumed bin liners!

RUTH: So this is the ship they say is unsinkable? Oh well, fingers crossed it's hijacked by terrorists, or this film's going to be piss boring.

4. EXT: POOP DECK – STUNSET

ROSE crosses the poop deck, flowing robes blowing in the wind, lit by a stunning sunset, or as it's known in the business, a stunset.

ROSE: I'm such a fool! Engaged to a hollow headed action man when Leonardo De Caprio is on the boat! I have to do something to attract his attention. . .

She begins to climb over the rail, when suddenly JACK appears behind her–

JACK: Wait! Don't do it!

ROSE: Er, don't come any closer or I'll jump!

JACK: Get real. You're the narrator.

ROSE: Okay then, what if I just slip off and dangle for a bit? Will you rescue me?

JACK: Whatever. . .

ROSE falls, dangles and begins to scream totally unconvincingly.

ROSE: Ahh, ahh, help me, help me, help me. Right, you can rescue me now.

JACK pulls her onto the deck, but she flops on top of him and starts to snog him.

ROSE: Oh no! I'm accidentally

snogging you!

Suddenly a voice calls out from close by. It's CAL.

CAL: Get your trotters off him Rose! He can't be more than ten years old!

ROSE: (urgent whisper) For God's sake, it's Leonardo De Caprio!

CAL: Ah! In that case, maybe the young gentleman would care to join us for dinner tonight. . . in first class!

5. INT: FIRST CLASS DINING ROOM – EVENING

JACK, ROSE, RUTH, CAL and VARIOUS PLUSH TOYS are sitting round a lavishly set table in the first class dining room.

RUTH: And where exactly do you live Mister Dawson? Dawson's Creek?

JACK: No. I work my way from place to place. Jumble sale here, dog's mouth there, sometimes I just tie myself to the grill of a lorry and see where it takes me.

RUTH: You find that sort of existence appealing do you?

JACK: I was made in China. I spent the first ten years of my life at the bottom of a grabbing machine in an arcade in Blackpool. I swore if anyone every won me I'd see the world and make every second count.

ROSE: (raising her glass) To every second counts! And to Paul Daniels for making it amongst the best gameshows on TV!

CAL: (to himself) The bear must die.

6. INT: THIRD CLASS PARTY ZONE – NIGHT

THIRD CLASS is alive with laughter, boozing, dancing, leprechauns, blarney stone kissing and other stereotypical Irish behaviour.

ROSE: This is amazing Jack! Is it always like this in third class?

JACK: Yes! Being poor is fantastic!

7. EXT: TOYTANIC PROW – STUNSET

It's another stunset. JACK and ROSE hold each other on the very tip of the prow.

JACK: Okay Rose. You can open your eyes now.

ROSE: (awestruck) Woah! I'm flying! What is this stuff?

JACK: PCP.

Suddenly a helicopter swoops down towards the boat, with 'Death From Above' painted on the side.

ROSE: What's that terrible noise?

JACK: Oh Shit! It's Celine Dion! Quick! Let's get outta here!

It is indeed everyone's favourite singing horse, Celine Dion, hovering above them in a helicopter. Loudhailer to her lips, she starts to wail her hideous THEME SONG.

8. INT: ROSE'S ROOM – NIGHT

JACK sits behind an artist's easel and ROSE is posed on a divan, nude but for the MEDALLION.

ROSE: I want you to draw me like one of your French girls.

JACK: What, you mean really badly?

ROSE: Yes. And totally nude.

She opens her legs and tips her head back languidly. There's nothing to see.

JACK: Where did you get that medallion?

ROSE: Jim gave it to me.

JACK: You mean Jim Cameron?

ROSE: No silly, Jimmy Saville! He fixed it for me to be in this film!

Up CLOSE, we see it is indeed a JIM'LL FIX-IT Medallion.

TO BE CONTINUED...

paul hogan meets hulk hogan

For years they have watched each other's careers from a distance, without ever speaking or meeting. Now, for the first time ever, the world's two most famous Hogans meet, and discuss film, their lives and their art.

PAUL HOGAN: Hi Hulk, good to meet ya.

HULK HOGAN: Hey dude, how are you?

PAUL: Wow, that's some handshake!

HULK: They don't call me Hulk for nothing!

PAUL: They sure don't! (Laughter). So let me start by saying I really admire your work. *Mister Nanny* is one of my favourite movies and I thought it was a really brave choice for you.

HULK: Well thanks, brother, I appreciate that. It was a tough movie to make, those kids sure were pesky and there were times when I found it hard not to snap their little bodies over my knee. May I say that I also admire your movie work very much. *Almost an Angel* is the only movie that ever made me cry. Were you disappointed when it didn't do too well at the box office?

PAUL: Well, Hulkster – may I call you Hulkster?

HULK: Just as long as I can call you Hogey.

PAUL: Be my guest, Hulkster. I'm sure you'll agree that box office receipts are no measure of the quality of a film. I'm still angry at the way they marketed that. It should have been a huge hit but the poster made it look like a film for queers. But let's go back to the beginning. The first time I became aware of you was when you fought Andre the Giant at *Wrestlemania Three*. I remember thinking, 'Wow, that guy has the same last name as me!'

HULK: Right, Hogey. I used to watch your show on TV, with all the girls with the great big titties, and I remember thinking exactly the same thing.

PAUL: Isn't that weird? And all this time we never thought of contacting each other.

HULK: Life is strange.

PAUL: You said it, mate.

HULK: And *Lightning Jack* is my favourite comedy Western of all time. It's such a great idea, a cowboy who's like a bumbling fool. I wish I'd thought of that!

PAUL: I've always wanted to ask you, how did you come up with the idea for *Thunder in Paradise*?

HULK: (Laughs) Yeah, it's a great title isn't it. I mean, who would expect thunder in Paradise? No-one. It should be sunny all the time in paradise, with a gentle breeze and plenty of shade. But we introduce the element of thunder, as if there's a storm on the way.

PAUL: But the Hulkster always catches the crims and keeps the sun shining!

HULK: You got it, brother!

PAUL: It's almost as if our careers have been intertwined. You were on top of the world when you won *Wrestlemania* in '84, around the same time they were lining up around the block for *Crocodile Dundee*...

HULK: That's right...and then when I defeated Macho Man for my second WWF title, you come back with *Crocodile Dundee Two* – wham – and it's even bigger than the first.

Craggy crocodile-monikered comedian and moustachioed musclebound mumbler – and both with the same surname! God sure moves in mysterious ways!

PAUL: Then we both went through difficult times in the early nineties. Can I ask you some personal questions, Hulk?

HULK: Depends what they are, little guy.

PAUL: I've read some pretty hurtful rumours about you which maybe you could clear up.

HULK: Oh-oh, here we go!

PAUL: Is it true you were born female?

HULK: No, it is not. That's a total bullshit lie. And if I found the guy who started that rumour he'd die a female, you better believe it, brother.

PAUL: Okay. Is it true that you suffer from clinical depression?

HULK: No, it is not true. I've never been happier. I mean, look at me sitting here talking face to face with Mick 'Crocodile' Dundee! How can I be depressed? Life can't get much better than this, can it?

PAUL: Amen to that. Hulkmania rules.

HULK: Alright brother. Can I ask you a personal question now?

PAUL: Go right ahead.

HULK: We're both famous for our headwear. You with your dangly cork hats and me with my bandanas. Does the constant cranial constriction ever bother you?

PAUL: Good question. Yes it does. Sometimes I'll take the hat off and it'll feel like I'm still wearing it. It's a strange sensation.

HULK: Wow, I have exactly the same thing... ∎

A&J'S USELESS C.V. GUIDE

Hear Ye! Hear Ye!

It is ye olde curriculum vitae of master

Joseph Flash Mulan Cornish

22 Nutbox Lane, East Henchley, London SE75
Date of Birth: 20.12.68 Sex: Male Nationality: British

Ye Education

1970 – 1974 Little Henchlings Nursery School
Excelled all-round in Primary Education, including flash cards, rice crispie cakes, potato printing, non-digital clock reading

1974–1982 St. Hench's Junior School
Achieved Beginner, Medium and Advanced BCG Swimming Certificates (including making floatation device from pants)
Inter-school Connect Four and Othello Champion '81
Prefect: Duties included checking all hands clean before lunch

1982–1987 Henchley House School for Boys
O Level Grades Achieved: English Language - B, English - C, Maths - C, History - C, Geography - D, Physics - E, Chemistry - U, Religious Education - D.
A Levels: English - C, History of Art - D, Practical Art - U.
Directed, produced and starred as Princess Leia in school play - The Star Wars Trilogy.

1988–1991 Frumpton College of Art and Design
BTEC Higher National Diploma in Confused Unsyllable Short Film Production
Advanced National Diploma in Deeply Confused Unsyllable Slightly Longer Film Production

---

1 Say no to novelty Using quirky coloured paper, high concept presentational ideas and fancy fonts, rather than making you 'stand out', only indicates that you are a raving ponce who's too desperate to be employable.

2 Two names are enough Putting your full name will always makes you sound like a sinister aristocrat who doesn't need any work anyway.

3 Forget your childhood No-one cares about what primary school you went to or what pathetic prizes you won there. Including such information will only make it seem like you're still the little twat you were back then.

4 Always lie It's a known fact that hardly any employers check the information on CVs. If they taught this in schools, it'd be the only lesson you'd ever need to learn. In fact, if they see crap results like this, rather than respect your honesty, they'll reject you straight off for not having the initiative to fib.

Ye Previous Employment

Summer '87 Spewster's Off Licence, Henchley High Street
Sales Assistant - Duties include operating till, handling cash, stealing stock. Won special commendation for confectionery display skills.

Summer '88 Bollockbuster Video, Henchley High Street
Sales Assistant. Responsibilities included putting wrong films in box, changing five pounds a night late fees, giving misleading advice, stealing stock.

Ye Hobbies And Interests

I enjoy relaxing, reading magazines, watching the television, eating and drinking, video games, smoking fags, snorkelling, scuba diving, windsurfing, pi-skiing, rollerblading, popular music, cinema, nightclubs, shopping, sunbathing, surfing the internet, chatting aimlessly, re-arranging my bits, staring into space, sleeping etc. etc.

Ye Foreign Travel

Have travelled extensively, including the Algarve, Corfu, the Algarve again, Disneyworld and also Portugal (Algarve). In my gap year I travelled to the exotic third world country of Thailand, where I subsisted in a bamboo hut for ten months on the remote, recently discovered island of Koh Samui.

Ye References

Mrs. A. Cornish
22 Nutbox Lane
East Henchley
London SE75

Mrs. B. Dawson
Careers Advisor
Toffington School
London W2

Tony Blair
Prime Minister
10 Downing Street
London W1

Ye Personal Statement

I am conscientious, hard-working, intelligent, very good looking, strong, well-dressed, sweet-smelling, ruthlessly ambitious, modest, enthusiastic, calm in a crisis, fully able to use my considerable initative, experienced in working as part of a team, have a great sense of humour, blend well into crowds and make a great cup of tea!!!!

I'M NO ORDINARY JOE, SO HIRE ME TODAY!!!

---

5 Forget your crap summer jobs They're not going to impress anyone except your dad, and then only at the time.

6 Hobbies are bad The more hobbies you have, the less time you'll be able to spend working and the more lazy you make yourself look.

7 Travelling is bad Who wants to know that you went to the third world in your year off? Everyone knows all you did is get amazingly stoned.

8 Get professional references Having your teachers or parents as referees is sad. Try and use people with proper jobs. Do not lie here though, this is the one thing they will check up on.

9 Forget your Personal Statement As if you're going to be objective. And never write one as if it was written by someone else about you. Everyone'll know you wrote it yourself and it's pure dogcrap.

10 Don't try and be funny Nothing revolts employers more than a sense of humour. It has been scientifically proven that no-one who puts jokes in their CV ever gets hired. And never mention your tea-making skills. You might as well write 'Help me, I'm crap.'

THE MAKING OF
SAVING PRIVATE RYAN

Sometimes the story behind a movie is just as extraordinary as the story of the movie itself. In these sensational excerpts from her new book, **Michelle Gayle** *describes the extraordinary events surrounding the development of Steven Spielberg's Oscar Winning war epic 'Saving Private Ryan'.*

The script for a major Hollywood movie can take more than twenty years to develop. Scores of writers may work on the material, combining the input of countless directors and producers who may be briefly attached to the project along the way. Steven Spielberg's 'Saving Private Ryan' is no exception. But what is exceptional is the identity of the very first man to come up with the story: Eastenders star Leslie Grantham.

Grantham is a handsome man, more so in the flesh than on television. When I ask him about his involvement in 'Saving Private Ryan', he sighs and stares up at the sky, a glimmer in his dirty blue eyes. "When I left Eastenders in 1986, my character Dirty Den was shot dead beside a canal. It was a depressing time for me, and I suddenly felt a deep affinity with the heroes of The Normandy Landings, many of whose lives also ended by being shot beside water. I decided to write a film that would capture what it would really have been like for those soldiers. So one weekend I took a ferry to France to visit the places where it actually happened. That's when I first became aware of Futuroscope."

These early 'Futuroscope' drafts of Private Ryan were very different from the film we know today. Instead of storming the Normandy beaches, Captain Miller and his men travelled to Futuroscope by coach-ferry-coach on an all-inclusive ticket purchased from London Waterloo. There they found Private Ryan enjoying a stunning 3-D film about

Captain Miller and his men arrived at Futuroscope by coach-ferry-coach on an all-inclusive ticket purchased from London Waterloo

undersea life on one of the largest Imax screens in the world. Although Grantham was pleased with his work, he felt it failed to capture the true essence of the Second World War.

Grantham passed his script onto old Eastenders colleague and friend Nick Berry (better known as 'Wicksey'), who worked on the script during breaks from filming 'Heartbeat'. "I told him to read it, not re-write it" Grantham recalls bitterly. But Berry did re-write it, inspired to take a radical new approach by ex co-star Anita Dobson. "I was playing a cameo role in Heartbeat" says Dobson, "and couldn't help noticing that Nick was spending every spare moment working on a script. I asked him what it was and he started telling me about the

Normandy Landings and Futuroscope. It didn't sound quite right to me, and that's when I suggested that maybe he should set it in EuroDisney instead."

Fuelled by this new idea, Berry wrote furiously, finally completing a four hundred page script set entirely in 'le Kingdom magique'. He gave copies to Grantham and Dobson and, crucially, Les Dennis, who happened to be visiting Dobson for the weekend. Dennis takes up the story. "Nick's work was amazing, very powerful, and you could see this was going to be a major film" says Dennis. "But I had my doubts about the EuroDisney element. Some of his descriptions of 'It's a Small World' were inaccurate, and the early scenes set on Big Thunder Mountain Railroad simply didn't do justice to the thousands of war veterans whose memory the film was to serve."

Dennis asked if he could have a shot at writing a draft. With nothing to lose, Berry agreed. He did not seek Grantham's permission. It was Dennis' draft, set entirely in Chessington World of Adventures, that was to first attract the attention of Steven Spielberg. "I'm a big fan of 'Give Your Mate a Break'," says Spielberg "and I'd been watching Les' career with interest for a while. I'd auditioned him years ago for the leads in 'Schindler's List' and 'The Colour Purple', and although he was very impressive, he wasn't right for either of those roles, but I made a mental note to work with him in the future'. Pleased with his Chessington draft, Dennis decided to send a copy to

The cast of Hollyoaks were put on standby, as were Balls Johnny and Zoe, Lennies Henry and Kravitz, the entire London company of 'Cats', and football hardman Vinny Jones

Spielberg, who read it and green-lighted the project virtually overnight. The one thing Dennis had forgotten to do, however, was to inform Berry, Dobson and Grantham. It was a mistake he would live to regret.

As well as being two of Britain's best loved comedians, Gareth Hale and Norman Pace also run Hollywood's best known casting agency, 'Spangles', from their Beckenham home. Dennis, a close friend, managed to persuade Spielberg to use 'Spangles' to cast 'Private Ryan'. Thrilled, Hale and Pace immediately called the top names on their books. The cast of Hollyoaks were put on standby, as were Balls Johnny and Zoe, Lennies Henry and Kravitz, the entire London company of 'Cats', and football hardman Vinny Jones.

"This was potentially a huge break for us,' says Pace. "Spielberg's a genius and a hard man to please, and we lost count of the times he sent us back to the drawing board," continues Hale. "But we finally had commitments lined up from Paul Daniels as Sgt. Miller, Adam Rickett as Private Ryan and Stuart from Blue Peter as the cowardly translator. Spielberg was happy and the whole project was ready to go." It was then that the famous director started to receive threatening phone calls from Grantham.

"I left message after message with his office explaining that Les' script had originated with me. All I ever got in return was verbal abuse from his security

staff. I couldn't take it anymore and I just snapped." Dobson had been out for dinner at Pizza hut in Leicester Square with Grantham, Dennis and Berry a few nights before. "Leslie was very angry with Les and Nick and me. Some very harsh words were exchanged. Eventually he said he was going to fly to Spielberg's house and 'sort him out.' There was no way any of us were going to let him go alone."

I t's impossible to construct a single consistent account of what happened outside Spielberg's front door the following night. "Leslie was very angry and determined," recalls Dennis. "He penetrated the security systems by brute force." The first thing he said to Spielberg when he opened the front door was 'No-one does the Dirty on Dirty Den.' Then it suddenly everything got very violent." "He hit me first," says Grantham. "Spielberg's a small man but he's also a martial arts expert, which I wasn't expecting."

"It all happened so fast," continues Dennis. "One minute Spielberg was standing there in his pyjamas, the next minute there were fists flying everywhere. I'm sure Leslie drew a knife at one point. I remember a flash of steel." "Yes, Leslie drew a knife, but thank God Nick got it off him before he did anything really stupid," remembers Dobson. "I was not carrying a knife and I never have carried a knife," asserts Grantham sternly today.

The fight was fast, desperate and brutal. Police reports state that Dobson removed a large clump of Spielberg's beard while trying to pull him off Grantham, who sustained serious bruising to his groin area. Les Dennis took the worst beating, suffering two broken wrists. Berry received several kicks to the face. Dennis, Dobson, Berry and Grantham spent the night in a downtown police cell. Berry claims Grantham said "home sweet home" as he was led inside, but Grantham denies it. "Don't be ridiculous. I never said that." The next morning, all four were put on the first flight to back England.

Keen not to fuel the flames of a scandal, Spielberg did not press charges. In return Dennis, Dobson, Berry and Grantham dropped all their claims on the script. Their names do not appear anywhere on the credits of 'Saving Private Ryan'. Spielberg brought in his own writers, who completely re-shaped the story, setting it on an actual beach. The only hint of Grantham's idea that remains is the thrill-ride style of the famous opening beach invasion. Much to Hale & Pace's disappointment, Spielberg discontinued his involvement with 'Spangles'.

Dobson removed a large clump of Spielberg's beard while trying to pull him off Grantham, who sustained serious bruising to his groin

Though all four stars want to put the incident behind them and all have plans to return to Hollywood, Grantham, Berry, Dennis and Dobson now no longer talk to each other. "If a lifetime hosting Family Fortunes has taught me anything, it's that we all make mistakes," says Dennis. Grantham is less philosophical. "That should have been me up there collecting that screenplay Oscar. If it hadn't been for my so-called showbiz friends and their so-called 'help,' my life would be totally different. I don't think I'll ever come to terms with it." Grantham is currently working on a film about the Bosnian War. "It's very graphic and realistic. It's set entirely at Blackpool Pleasure Beach. Phil Schofield read it and he says he's going to show it to Quentin Tarantino," he tells me. Isn't he afraid of history repeating itself, I ask? He allows himself a sardonic chuckle. "No. No way. If one good thing's come out of this mess, it's that the world knows never to do the Dirty on Dirty Den."

STREET SCORING

NOTE: Adam and Joe in no way condone the buying, selling or consumption of grade B illegal substances, unless you can get them some while you're at it.

It's a sad reflection on contemporary society that the vast majority of young people will, at some point, attempt to buy soft drugs on the street. It can take up to five years for them to find a dealer who can come round to their house, or someone at work who supplies. So to avoid wasting your hard-earned cash on tea leaves or a knife in the ribs, take note of these common soft-drug rip-off street scams.

THE FAKE GEAR SCAM

If you're young, respectable and stupid looking, most street dealers will try to palm you off with fake gear. The simplest way for them to do this is to rub real hash onto a piece of slate or liquorice to give it the correct aroma. Alternatively they show you some real pot, then exchange it for a small lump of dogshit. More sophisticated methods include letting you have a 'sample' pull on the real joint they're smoking, rendering you instantly soft-headed, then selling you a bag of mixed herbs.

THE 'POLICE' PRESSURE MOVE

Any dealer worth his salt will open transactions with a warning about the high number of undercover cops in the area. He will urge you to do the deal quickly whilst emphasising that the stuff he's about to sell you is quite the best in history. If you try to inspect the goods too closely, he'll make like the police are closing in at that very moment. The genius of this scam is that it's almost always true, and you can never be totally sure that it isn't.

THE 'SAFER WITH A FRIEND' MYTH

Everyone knows that street scoring alone is a big no-no. You should always take a friend with you. But don't kid yourself that this makes you any safer. Your friend is bound to be just as weedy as you, and the idea that somehow two of you are more likely to overpower a large professional criminal with a knife than one of you is frankly misplaced. If he wants to rip you off at knifepoint, he will, however many of you there are. Your friend is there to share your fear, no more, no less.

THE BASIC 'IDIOT' SCAM

You pass a dealer, make eye contact, and he leads you up an alley to do the deal. You discuss details of quantity and cost, then he tells you to give him the money and wait a couple of minutes while he goes and gets the gear. You do as he says, and end up standing on the street corner for an hour until either it dawns on you that you've been roundly suckered, or a policeman arrives to bust you. An hour later you run into him again and he makes like he doesn't know you. You get indignant, he stabs you in the face.

THE 'INSURANCE' SCAM

An evolution from the Basic Idiot Scam. This time when the dealer tells you to give him the money up front, you refuse. He starts to get angry, accusing you of not trusting him, saying the cops are closing in as you speak. But you've learned from experience and you hold your ground. Finally he comes up with an idea. He pulls a baggie of white powder from his pocket and tells you it's his entire stash of cocaine. He will give it to you to hold as insurance while he goes and gets his grade-B substances. Being an amateur, you're impressed by the powder, and agree to the deal. Even if he never comes back with the soft drugs, you'll have a bag of hard stuff to impress your mates with, you think. Off the dealer trots with your money, never to return. The powder, as you discover at two in the morning when you attempt to snort it in a vain attempt to get over your pot cravings, is crushed aspirin.

THE GUN-FREE CAR-JACK

This time you've borrowed your parents' car for the night, packed it full of mates and driven to that seedy area of town where soft drugs are sold. You make eye contact with a dealer and he indicates that you should pull up round the corner. He approaches your car at the driver's window and you wind it down to greet him. This is your first and last mistake. Before you know it, his hand darts inside the car and grabs hold of the keys in the ignition. Now he threatens to run away with the keys unless you give him all your money. You have no option but to pay up, and your evening is buggered. Time to just go and get drunk like everyone else.

DRUGS. JUST SAY NO, THANKS ANYWAY, NOT REALLY. GOT ANY HOOCH?

Dr Fischer Verlag's
Encyclopedia Of Partial Medicine
PART ONE: SPOTS

Good day there. My name is Doktor Hans Fischer Verlag and I am an expert. Today I tackle the common problem of spots. You may have been out of your teens for quite sometime now, but if like me, you are on a strict sweets and crisps diet you may still suffer occasionally from pubescent outbreaks of spotting. I am not going to tell you how to cure these as I don't know; I just want to frighten you if you haven't started getting them yet. Here's a few you can expect...

THE DEEP IMPACT

This spot seems to be growing inwards to create a painful 'new muscle' on the face and never seems to come to a head. Trying to squeeze the Deep Impact will result in minutes of eye watering strain followed, after a three-second pause, by agonisingly sharp pain.

THE DANTE'S PEAK

Seems innocent enough until you try squeezing, then... KABOOM! You have to get a new mirror. These are, in truth, a lot of fun and extremely satisfying, just like the Linda Hamilton film of the same name. Unless they then start to bleed afterwards in which case your evening will be a self-conscious mop-a-thon.

THE GLASTONBURY

A whole group of tiny white heads jostling each other uncomfortably. Attempting to squeeze this outcrop would be about as productive as trying to straighten grass.

THE RUDOLPH

The painfully bulbous beacon that grows at the very tip of your nose and makes it impossible for anyone to conduct a conversation with you without first mentioning 'the spot'. It feels like a hot lightbulb and yes, you could even say it glows.

HOW SPOTS MIGHT WORK

To be honest I am unclean and unclear as to why skin blemishes and ugly lesions occur, I just know they do. Science has shown that their appearance is linked to important occasions, like going for a hot sex-possibility type date or meeting Matthew Kelly. I don't know what this diagram means.

Should be a good one.

wANKST

Come on you worthless little tossers, pour out your drivel, send it in and we'll print it.

I AM RIGHT AND YOU ARE WRONG... WHY DON'T YOU AGREE WITH ME?...THIS BAND IS GOOD, THAT BAND IS BAD... YOUR ARTICLE MADE ME ANGRY...I FEEL LONELY

FOINTING THE PINGER

I have just finished reading Steve Shelfin's so-called 'comments' about Fointy Pinger (Wankst, October 8th) and I feel I have to express my outrage and disbelief. Is he really implying that Matt & Luke Futch are encouraging violence with their song 'You Like Fist Punch'? It's IRONIC you witless shit-for-brains peepee stain! But I'm being silly, you're a Runcorn fan, you wouldn't know irony if it came up and crapped on your mother's face, you worthless pube collector! If you want to go around accusing bands of encouraging violence, why don't you look closer to home, you hideous nut-smelling vomitgibbon. Runcorn's woeful ratshit of an 'album' is stuffed with thinly-veiled calls to arms that would embarrass Adolf fuckbox Hitler!! What the spunking hell is 'Needle Duvet' if not a direct incitement not only to violence, but ethnic cleansing, and nuclear war?! Go and clean up your own shitfilled backyard before you start chucking your stinking ignorant pony toss at real bands like Fointy Pinger whose feet you could only dream of wanking over, you lonely bogey burglar.

ELEANOR HUSK, E-MAIL

It's all very well making ironic statements about serious issues, but what happens when those comments are NOT ironic? Then you have just statements and that spells DANGER. Enough people thought 'You Like Fist Punch' was pro-punch for it to be an issue which then means they should apologise, which they have not. – DS

CHURCH OF THE POISONED MIND

I love your magazine but one thing does trouble me with it. What have you got against Franjeeson Nielson? He is the best thing that ever happened in my life! His album *The Dirty Church Of Franjeeson Nielson* made me understand that organised religion is evil and that until we ban all religions there will never be peace in the world. I am not alone in thinking this because I have been to 5 Franjeeson Nielson concerts and there are literally dozens of people who love his music and believe his messages. If you don't like him, then why don't you just leave him alone? Saying his album sounds like 'a long fart in a tiny cupboard' is not true and shows you as bullies. I am writing this from across the road and I can see you all in the window. I don't want to hurt anyone but if you do not stop saying these things you will be surprised. I like the cartoon in your magazine.

PORL SHORLEY, ROAD

I personally have not criticised Franjeeson Nielson – DS

BLAH BLAH BLAH

How much longer are we expected to collaborate in the conspiracy to canonise Banned Name? Their woeful sub-Fundle sludge is not remotely as original as say, the first God's Box Of Sox album or anything by The Buggernauts. Stop wanking over them this instant or I'll come round and puke on all your Gripps bootlegs!

DANIEL SHITT, BLAH

Thankyou, thankyou, thankyou for getting me into Banned Name! Before reading about this brilliant band I was a total arsehole, but now I have met a girl called Deborah who also loves Banned Name! Their music is better than any of the other bands and anyone who disagrees is an arsehole! Will you be writing about Banned Name again in the magazine? Their album *Cold Blue Fachunka* was the best album of last year! I hate Fointy Pinger. Also Rick Trickle from New Sage Gent is an arsehole.

PETRA MEKON, NORTH JIP

Hideon Rickles from Banned Name will be in the What Do You Like And What Do You Not Like section next week. – DS

SOME MORE PISH

I am a Sinking Moons fan and proud of it and, to be frankly honest, I am utterly and totally pissed off with Greg Joint's review of their 'Best Of' album (*Now! Music! Now!*, May 22). I get the impression he just listened to the songs and wrote down the first thing that came into his head about them, just like the other scumbag pseudo-intellectual twat journalists who have written them off recently. So what if they just cover jingles from Tampon commercials, they still have more originality in their little fingers than Chanty Aunty, Killerbox and Stinkywatch put together, I think. What I want is more people saying they're good and less people saying they're bad. So it's a one fingered salute to Greg Joint and a turbo charged huzzah! to The Sinking Moons.

PS. This letter took me ages to write and I am very pleased with it.

KIERON STIERON, SLUPP

Edited by Denny Splazz

NU SHOEBILLY: THE DEBATE RAGES ON

Nu Shoebilly is the worst pile of shite in the world and you are all c***s for writing about it in your shitty mag. Fuck all of you. I bet you don't print this letter.

BILL FIST, MUTTONPILE, HOCKS

The Stompin' Plowpeople rule! Nu Shoebilly rules! I wish all music was exactly the same as Nu Shoebilly! Is there a specialist shop selling accessories? If not I will build one.

GEORGIA SKIRT, BILTONG

Will the girl with green dreads at the Stompin' Plowpeople gig at The Yertl last wednesday please get in touch. I stole your jacket but I don't want it now.

JIM GROWTH, TENT

PS WE HAVE TO FILL THIS BIT TOO. . .

Almost four months after the third Sludgemore Indiefest in Frottermaster, Wankst is still being inundated, nay, bombarded with complaints by the arseload about the poor quality of the event. "The rain was consistent and went on mostly for hours," writes Lilo Godfrit of Bilge. "My tent was wet and my clothes got wet. It was uncomfortable and there was nowhere to get away from all the people."

A similar tale comes via the web from Justin McConville-Rugger from Chickle who says, "I won't be going back in to the festival. The band I like, Lazer Fuckstick, did not sound like they did on the record I bought. Me and my friends wanted them to play 'Headfuck (You Give Me A)' but I'm fairly sure they didn't. We had to queue for beer which we then had to pay for and later the girl I accidentally got some sick on was furious. Why can't people just get along at festivals, I thought that was the point."

Ned Parsley who owns the relatively old Sludgemore Manor where the festival takes place, responded to criticism of the event thusly: "Sludgemore is the most eagerly anticipated event in my calendar. Things go wrong. If people don't like it they should keep quiet. I can control the rain, but it all costs money, and that means fewer burgers and worse music. Next year I suggest people complain less and pay more or I may decide to shut the gates altogether but force the groups to play anyway, to teach the children a lesson in manners. That's all."

But the last word goes to Kimberly Frig who writes, "Where can I get cheap drugs?"

21st Century POP!

NEW KIDS ON THE BLOCK!

Fflupp! Has your Pop gone flat? Get ready to meet the components of the musical Sodastream that's going to pump the fizz back in 'til the bottle blows! Shazzaam! Denny Splazz picks out tomorrow's favourite flavours, and cherry isn't one of them! Woppit!

FOINTY PINGER

"Angry? Angry? We're fucking furious," spits Fointy Pinger frontman Matt Futch. "Britain's a cocking mess and no one gives a shit. People can't be arsed with anything except doing another line and forgetting everything. We're the rock 'n' roll alarm clock that's going to wake you bastards up again and get you buzzing on four-star adrenalin instead of lines of Vim."

The new millennium is upon us and neo-punk Orfington three-piece Fointy Pinger are ready to punch it's lights out! Frustrated by the apathy of youth culture The Pingers are kicking against the pricks with bitter tirades of vivid venom and beautiful bile, fuelled by seven-inch bursts of lipsmackin' bodyslammin' pop and breathtaking arrogance. Their third single 'Loose Eye' out this week on the Strentford based Goink label comes on like the bastard son of Saundbahn and The Jennifer Suggestion locked in a room with Nasty Basket and forced to listen to Jolts out-takes!

"We're constantly inspired by the mediocrity of our contemporaries" sneers Matt's brother and lead guitarist Luke Futch. "They're not fit to lick the Sunny Delight off our boots and they know it! I mean, no wonder this country's in such a state when all the teenagers have to listen to is Frotten and The Windscream Vipers. Fuck me, how can people accept such mediocrity when Shouty Shitz got 'Shaggin' Maggie Thatch' to number one?" One thing's for certain, if Fointy Pinger have their way, this is the year you're gonna find the hell out!

Key Track So Far: '(We hate it when people put song titles in) Brackets'

splush

You're at a really shit party in the middle of nowhere. Everyone except you knows each other and won't talk to you and the friend you came with has got pissed and buggered off with your keys and your wallet. You're just trying to find someone with a phone so you can call a minicab that won't come for an hour and a half, if they can find the place at all, when the pill you got off the dodgy looking bloke who's just passed out in the lav starts kicking in. Suddenly, in the midst of this godawful crapstorm, you realise you don't give a shit anymore! You are indestructible, an 80 foot sculpture of stainless steel genius towering above the filth and the fury in cloudless space, your mind slipping it's surly bonds and soaring out towards the edges of the solar system, never to return to it's prison head. Then you throw up. And that's Splush.

Formed last year in a greasy spoon in Depreicester, Andy Yott (vocals, guitar, moog), Faz Hugley (moog, vocals, moog) and Brendan Ishtar (moog, dreams, spangle) and Gillingham Dreft (old records, moog, coffee, flipcharts) make music that pretends the rest of the world doesn't exist. But transcendant elliptical melodies and achingly beautiful vocal stylings are only half of the oh-so extraordinary picture, as Andy Yott explains.

"We aren't interested in being like those other bands. All we care about is being the best band on the planet. That's why we wear suits. We're in business of making music that no one's ever heard before." prepare yourselves for the Splush corporation, where business is good. Business is very good.

Key Track So Far: Are You Brenda Blethyn?

.. THE PESTLE IN THE VESSEL .

Trying to pin down the noise made by this bunch of Hoebench-On-Tea scamps is like trying to get a cat into a crisp packet. You shouldn't really do it but it's fun having a go! Songs like 'Scared Of Your Head' and 'Big Delicious Killer' from their 'Brew That Is True' EP sound like The Reminders singing B-sides by The Kitchen Towels while T.J. Hookah scratches early Jennifer Suggestion over the top, on acid!

So where does the sound come from? 'We grew up in a really big house and went to very expensive schools,' explains The Pestle's Lilo Gurfin, 'and that can really fuck you up. People think it's all champagne and debutantes but that's only part of it. Sometimes you get bored and our music comes from copying other bands when we're bored.' And aren't they worried about being written off as posh no-talent chancers? "Yes, we are actually," muses bassist Ollie Popcork. "I really wish Lilo hadn't just told you all that. We got a stylist in specially to make us look a bit more downmarket and now he's ballsed it all up.'
Key Track So Far: Wotcher Star Monkey!

NEOSONIQUE

Unless you were hiding in your Dad's spare tube of Anusol all last year (Spatchcock!) you'll already be familiar with the twisted space-metal cum techno-blues-funk of Neosonique. Yes, it was these Belgian nob twiddlers that remixed the everlovin' shiz out of Le Jardin Du Fax Modem's 'Road Sandwich' and Noncepockits' surprise number one club stomper 'Smelly Under Watch'. Success in their own right was slower coming, with a disappointing reception for their excellent debut single 'Brint' and the follow up 'Your Goitre' despite constant airplay from Glyn Squatt's instore music showcase on MFI FM.

But if you were planning to ignore the new album, 'Ne Touche Pasta', then you'd better make some new plans that don't include ignoring the new album, 'Ne Touche Pasta'. Quite simply it's the kind of 21st century pan-galactic Bagpuss-meets-Quatermass in a pitch invasion mindfuck that Lilt Fridge always promised but never quite delivered, and with critics on both sides of the office already calling it the album of the year it could well be a contender for album of the year.

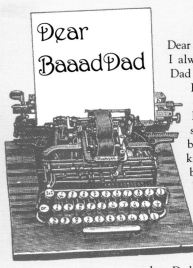

Dear BaaadDad

Dear BaaadDad,
I always loved my Mum and Dad very much but recently I've been seeing a whole different side of them that I can't stand. They always say they just want what's best for me but how do they know? They think my boyfriend is a 'creep' just because he has a pierced eyebrow but they don't even make the effort to see all the good things about him. He came round the other day and my Dad was so sarcastic and rude it really upset me. If I did that to one of their boring friends they would kill me. At least I don't spend all my time arguing over pathetic things like they do. I feel like I've discovered they are the real creeps. Why are they like that? *Marie, 14*

MARIE. *Ironically, your mum and dad are "like that" because they love you and react with suspicion, even with hostility, to what seems to them a threat to your wellbeing. It almost certainly isn't just the pierced eyebrow that turns them off your boyfriend. To them, this harmless vanity suggests the possibility of other, far from harmless, things which – wrongly – they imagine to be inseparable from such trendy superficialities; things like drugs and sexual promiscuity; even petty crime. What you are experiencing in their behaviour is not hostility for hostility's sake, but anxiety, even fear, that the daughter they love may be at risk. As to what you can do about it – see my reply to Sholana, below.*

Dear BaaadDad,
My friends all take drugs but I never have and more and more I feel left out when they get stoned. They say I should try smoking grass because it's not as dangerous as pills or coke and better for you than alcohol but I've heard people say it gets you onto harder drugs. Surely it can't hurt to try it at least once? Every singer I like seems to smoke it and they seem fine. *Dominic, 15*

DOMINIC. *Informed and learned debate as to the harmfulness, or otherwise, of "soft" drugs appears to be endless and wholly inconclusive. The chances are that trying grass "at least once" would indeed do you no great harm; the trouble is, you can't be sure. Is it worth the risk? You asked for my opinion, so* here it is. Carry on feeling "left out" when your friends get stoned: your reward may be to be left out also when they are being incarcerated in a drug rehabilitation clinic.

Dear BaaadDad,
I am a fifteen year old boy who thinks he might be gay. I've snogged a couple of girls but I didn't really fancy them. There's a boy in school who is really nice and a good mate but when he touches me or brushes up against me I get really turned on. I don't think he feels the same way and if any of my mates knew what I was thinking they'd probably take the piss. Plus my parents would go mental because I've heard them say it's unnatural and a sin and that all gay people are lonely and unhappy, but I don't feel evil and I've got lots of mates. I'm so scared. I just want to be happy but I don't think the way I feel is just a phase. Should I tell my parents and friends, I don't know what to do. *Steven, 15*

STEVEN. *This is a really tough one. The fact that your parents may have said what you say they have said about gay people does not necessarily mean that they would "go mental" if you told them about your own problem. But it's a risk you might have to take. What's the alternative? If there is a teacher at your school whom you like and get on well with you might do far worse than to talk to him, or her. What is certain is that in order that you may not "go mental" you must talk with someone. If you really are gay (and nothing you have described proves that conclusively), then the sooner you start coming to terms with it, the better.*

Dear BaaadDad,
I'm sick of people telling me the way I dress is wrong or a joke. I'm a Marilyn Manson fan and I paint my face white, have a lot of piercings and wear very high orthopedic boots. I think the way I look expresses who I am and it doesn't hurt anyone so why are people so horrible, always calling me names like 'monkeyfreak' or 'wonkybox' and pointing at me. Why should be like everyone else? I think they are the ones who look ridiculous. *Tanya, 17*

TANYA. *If you choose to draw attention to yourself by going against all convention in ways that many people would consider freakish you ought neither to be surprised, nor offended, if you are treated as something of a freak by being pointed at and called freakish names. It takes a certain kind of courage to look the way you evidently do; now be consistent and take the horrible reactions of the rest of us boringly orthodox observers on your white-painted chin. Words needn't hurt you.*

Dear BaaadDad,
My parents are always putting me down and I can't stand it any more. They hate the way I look (I recently shaved my head),and they hate the music I love but won't even try to understand it. They are always going on about how kids these days have 'gone off the rails and have too much freedom' but it doesn't feel like it to me. I work really hard and do well at school and I only do drugs occasionally, so what's the problem? Why can't they chill out and be nice for a change?   Sholana, 16

SHOLONA. *For your parents to "chill out and be nice" would require the abandoning on their part of a host of prejudices and convictions ("principles", they would call some of them) acquired over their whole lifetimes. It's too much for you to ask. But here you have a wonderful opportunity to demonstrate what seems to me one of the really marvellous characteristics of contemporary youth; its tolerance. Smile when people talk about kids going "off the rails" and you know very well that you are firmly on them.Carry on working hard. Don't do drugs at all. Hold your shaven head high (But don't paint it!). Don't play your music too loudly. Don't argue. And finally, be patient: your parents will grow out of their ill-advised attitudes in time.*

Dear BaaadDad,
A few weeks ago in gym class I had to climb the rope and half way up I started to get a strange feeling around my groin. Now I sometimes sneak into the gym to climb the rope when no one is around to get the feeling again. Sometimes my shorts are damp afterwards. I keep thinking about it all the time. Am I sick? I don't know what's wrong with me.
                              Martin, 12

MARTIN *You are not sick and there is nothing whatever wrong with you. Very simply, the movements involved in climbing the rope are resulting in a form of sexual experience, the "strange feeling" being exactly the same sensation that boys older than you are able to experience by what may delicately be called "pleasuring" themselves, or crudely (I understand) is sometimes known as "jerking off" – in a more proper word, masturbation. So don't worry and go on climbing; sex will never be so trouble-free again.*

Dear BaaadDad,
All my friends are snogging girls but I still haven't snogged anyone. I know it's because I am quite ugly but I'm not the ugliest person in the school and I think I'm nicer than a lot of the more handsome blokes. The girl I really like is going out with this older guy who treats her really badly and he just gets away with it because he's older and has a car. He's not even that good looking and he's thick. I wish I could change the way I look but I can't, so does that mean I'm going to be alone all my life unless I go out with other ugly people?   Jason, 15

JASON. *No man is the best judge of what he himself looks like in the eyes of other people, especially not in the eyes of the opposite sex. Superficially, women may be attracted by obvious good looks. In the long run they are far more concerned with what is behind the face that the world sees. Humour; kindness; intelligence; intellectual ability; and of course money and power, all rate far higher in a worthwhile woman's estimate of a man than do skin-deep appearances. Truly ugly, physically repellent men are as hard to find as gold nuggets on Brighton beach. I very much doubt that you have that distinction.*

BUILD YOUR OWN A&J BEDROOM!

INSTRUCTIONS

1) Take this book to a colour copier shop, or to work, if you've got one there.
2) Copy these two pages. Enlarge them if you feel like it.
3) Stick the copies onto white card and cut out the three bits with pictures on.
4) Glue the two sides onto the back and fold inwards slightly so the diroama will stand up.

The Footie Song

TACTICS FOR MATCH
FOOT - BALL - BALL
BALL - FOOT - KICK
FOOT - KICK - BALL
KICK - BALL - FOOT
BALL - GOAL !
WE WIN BALL !

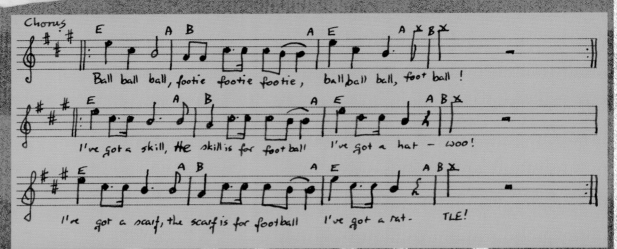

Chorus

Ball ball ball, footie footie footie, ball ball ball, foot ball !

I've got a skill, the skill is for football   I've got a hat — woo!

I've got a scarf, the scarf is for football   I've got a rat- TLE!

Chorus:
Ball, ball, ball,
Footie, footie, footie,
Ball, ball, ball,
Football!

Repeat chorus

I've got a skill
The skill is for football
I've got a hat
Wool!

I've got a scarf
The scarf is for football
I've got a rat-
-tle!

Chorus

When I go see United
I get over excited
When I go see Millwall
I know I'll see a good game of
football

When I go see Tottenham
I know there'll be no stoppin'em
When I go see Spurs
If it's cold and Debbie's got a
hat I'll borrow hers

Chorus

When the game's beginning
All the crowd start singing
When the goals start scoring
It becomes less boring

When I go see Arsenal
I reckon they can pass'n'all
When I go see Villa
My view is blocked by a concrete
pillar

Chorus

All the teams wear numbers
Ironed onto their jumpers
Strips are different colours
It helps you sort out one from the
others

When the game gets dirty
The ref becomes all shirty
When the teams change ends
It's time to talk tactics with my
friends

Chorus

Here we go—
G-L-E-N-H-O-D-D-L-E-I-S-H-A-V-I-
N-G-A-G-O-A-L
Glenn Hoddle is having a goal!
Foot, foot, foot, foot, ball
Ball, ball, ball, ball, foot,
Kick, kick, kick, kick, foot
Foot kick ball — goal!

Chorus

When I go see Rovers
I wear my Rovers pullovers
When I go see Leeds
They seem to achieve a lot of high
ball speeds

When I go see Nottingham
There don't half seem like a lotta
them
When I go see Chelsea
Spend half the match in the queue
for a wee wee

Repeat Chorus

Foot-foot-foot-
toot-football!

Adam & Joe's HOROSCOPE

aries

You will acquire special powers in your eyes that allow you to see through the clothes of ladies. Even if you are a lady. Sadly it won't work on men.

taurus

Take more care in video shops. You have a tendency to think "Hey! This one's got two sequels! The sequels are probably shit, but the original has got to be good!" That is bad videologic. Get out *Groundhog Day* again. You can't go wrong.

gemini

Why don't you wank each other off? I would.

cancer

Your best feature is your nose. Never too runny, always on time. Consider purchasing some kind of device to wear on your head that covers your face and reveals only your nose. You could put small lights on it to make the nose even more glamourous. They could flash.

leo

If you're honest with people, 9 times out of 10 they will thank you for it. To this extent honesty is the best policy. Some things, however, are better left unsaid. Honesty should not necessarily compel you to tell people you find them ugly or boring. This is the 1 time out of 10 you would be well advised to shut your stupid mouth.

virgo

This month you will start to over-use the word 'pop'. "I'm just going to pop to the shops", "Can you pop it over there?", "Pop your top off for me love" etc. Stop the pop and try talking prop.

libra

For someone who is supposedly so 'balanced' you certainly are a fucking mess.

scorpio

What an exciting month for you both! Also you will travel back through time and compose the century's greatest pop tunes one month before they were written and take credit for them, establishing yourself as the greatest musician of the 20th century. This actually happened to Nick Kershaw but he was a big Howard Jones fan and took credit for a load of real shit.

sagittarius

A last-minute change of plans this month leads to an opportunity to visit an old friend who gives you some unexpected news which enables you to pursue a new path which will eventually lead you back to square one.

capricorn

Blah blah blah.

aquarius

Don't move. Stay perfectly still. Just behind you, about 3 feet to your left there is a huge spider that came in a box of foreign fruit. It has teeth and can stand upright. It's name is Stevo.

pisces

Fed up to the gills with friends fishing for compliments, swimming in cod sincerity? Can't find a plaice to perch? Sick of whiting in roes? Gap in your love life and carping for salmon to fillet? Feeling eel? See a sturgeon. I'm sorry.

RULES OF THE CINEMA

The nerdy jobsworth usher cannot deviate from the commands of the central ticketing computer. So even though the cinema is empty, he seats you in the middle of the middle block, with five strangers.

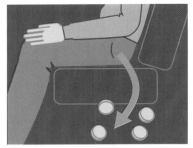

Upon sitting down, all your small change will fall out of your pockets and roll away.

There will be 45 minutes of adverts before the film, every single one of which is on TV at the moment.

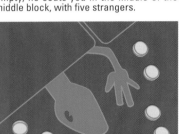

According to the warning to keep hold of valuables, there is a slithering snake thief guy who lives under the seats. This is true.

Next to you will be a guy with a very strange breathing problem, who also breaks wind disgustingly at regular intervals.

If you try to move, the usher will swoop and insist you sit back in your allocated seat. Sorry sir, company policy.

As soon as the film starts, someone will come in late. Their mate will stand up to shout and whistle as they wander around stupidly, before falling over you.

Behind you will be someone who pushes, kicks and jolts the back of your seat until it becomes more like an Imaginator ride.

There will be a guy who repeats every half-decent line of dialogue and then laughs very loudly. "You've been erased! Didja hear that? Erased! Ha ha ha ha!"

Every screening will also include someone translating and explaining every word and action in the movie for their foreign friends.

The tallest man in the world will sit in front of you. He has a sore back and cannot slump properly.

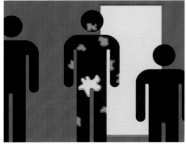

Upon leaving, you will be covered in melted Maltesers and have Coke dribbles all down your leg.

A&J's GUIDE TO THE OWNERSHIP OF LIGHTERS

CLASS A: transparent plastic and mini disposables

Do not become attached to these lighters. Despite their Tardis-like capacity and longevity they belong to whoever picks them up. You do not have a case for holding on to a CLASS A lighter.

Thus: **"Have you got my lighter?"**
"I've got THE lighter, you tight goink."

CLASS B: disposables featuring a design

(Polkadots, stripes, "Dicken's Bar-Thaxos", World Cup football players, naked ladies, Clive Gibbons from Neighbours etc.)
There is a case for a CLASS B lighter having sentimental value. It is rather a sad case though so think hard before saying: **"Have you got my lighter?"**
"The one you think proves you've been to New York? I suppose I do."

CLASS C: refillable & novelty items

(Zippos, guns, phones, cougars with red eyes, cars, naked ladies etc.)
Refillability = Commitment. Refillability + Novelty = Long-term Commitment. Despite the fact that these seldom refill satisfactorily ('Oooh! My thumb's gone all frosty') and are lost easily, the CLASS C lighter should not be stolen. If found please return to owner. **"Have you got my firebreathing Godzilla lighter?"**
"I was merely admiring the craftsmanship."

CLASS D: posh lighters

(Cartiers, long golden cylinders, marble blocks, anything on a big leather topped desk)
What are you doing spending that much on a lighter you silly toilet? Are you the head of an evil conglomerate? You are not. In fact you are playing Summer Of '69 by Bryan Adams very loudly in your open topped Jag on the King's Road. So: **"Have you got my lighter?"**
"No, I don't have any charlie."

THE BRAIN OF KEN

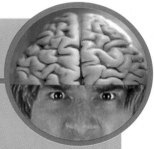

Got an impossible film trivia question that no-one down the pub can answer? Got a movie moment indelibly imprinted on your memory but can't remember what film it was in? Ken Korda, the man with the solid celluloid brain, is here to set you straight.

DEAR KEN
I once saw a film on TV in which an English Nobleman is captured by the Sioux Indians and forced to undergo a savage initiation ceremony. At one point I recall him being hung from the ceiling by hooks through his nipples.   *Ben Stain – Mancs*

DEAR BEN
The film you saw starred Robert Carlyle as an unemployed steelworker who starts a male strip troupe, and was called 'The Full Monty'. It's widely considered the greatest comedy of all time.

DEAR KEN
Can you identify an old family film about a trio of kids with a railway line at the foot of their garden? At one point a young Jenny Agutter stops a train by ripping off her skirt and waving it the air.   *Sven Morris, Kent*

DEAR SVEN
The film you describe is the hilarious world-wide hit comedy 'The Full Monty', starring Robert Carlyle as an unemployed steelworker who starts a male strip troupe. How lucky you are to have this ninety minutes of pure joy to look forward to!

DEAR KEN
As a child, I remember sneaking into my parents room late at night and being scared to death by the climax of a the movie they were watching, in which a man shot a woman in the face at point blank range with a creamy white fluid. Was I dreaming or does this film exist?   *Len Webber, Notts*

DEAR LEN
Yes it does exist. It was made in 1997 and starred Robert Carlyle as an unemployed steelworker who starts a male strip troupe. It's called 'The Full Monty', and you may be able to find a copy of it on video if you're lucky. Happy hunting!

LONDON'S PREMIERE WEST END THEATRE   ADMISSION ALWAYS GUARANTEED

THE OLD EMPORIUM THEATRE

64 COBBLERS STREET, LONDON W1

EXCLUSIVE WEST END PRESENTATION*

NEAREST TUBE: LAVVY LANE   HOME OF THE FAMOUS 'SCANTY SISTERS'

*EXCLUDING SCHOOLS, PRISONS & OIL RIGS

WESTMINSTER COUNCIL OFFICIAL RECEIVERS PRESENT
CHARLIE SPRACKETT'S 'TIMELESS CLASSIC'
IF YOU LOVED 'OLIVER' YOU'LL QUITE LIKE

BOBO!

THE BOB HOSKINS STORY

Starring BOB HOSKINS as himself

and
From TV's 'Stop It Mum'
TODDY PIPKINS
as 'Fidget'

With
Former Olympic Skate Star
JANE STENCH
as 'Fanny'

And
BARRY WILMOTT
as 'Sniper Hawkins'

**FEATURING
SUCH WELL-LOVED
SONGS AS:**
'Song For Bob Hoskins'
'Ooga Booga!'
'Loverly Fanny!'
'Naff Off!'
'It's Good to Talk'
'I've never put a better
bit of butter on me
knife!'

Produced by BOB HOSKINS
Directed by BOB HOSKINS,
WESTMINSTER COUNCIL
OFFICIAL RECEIVERS and
FIXIT LTD

**THE CRITICS
SING ABOUT
'BOBO!'**
'...jaw droppingly...'
'....music...set
design...'
'...quite extraordinary
dancing...'
'...very tense...'
'...children... crying...
laughter....'
'...tragic...'
'...clean, attractive toilets...'

APPEAR IN 'BOBO!'
– ASK AT THE BOX
OFFICE.

ASK ABOUT OUR
TEN-FOR-ONE TICKET
OFFER!

ORIGINAL CAST ALBUM
AVAILABLE SOON ON
'NICE PRICE'

RETAIN YOUR TICKET STUB FOR
DISCOUNT ENTRY INTO
WESTMINSTER COUNCIL PUBLIC
CONVENIENCES

Throughout my life, people of all ages have constantly come up to me asking about my career. 'Tell us a story about the making of Super Mario Brothers!' they'll say, or 'were you supposed to be American in Roger Rabbit?', or 'what's Dexter Fletcher really like?' This musical is my way of answering all those questions.

It tells my life story from my birth in the East End at the turn of the century, through my early days as England's youngest human cannonball, right through to the making of my directorial debut 'The Raggedy Rawney'. I hope you enjoy watching my life as much as I've enjoyed living it, and don't be afraid to sing along!'

TODDY PIPKINS (Fidget)
Toddy Pipkins trained at the Todd Cartey Stage School and made his TV debut as the little boy in the popular Werther's Original commercials. 'Bobo' marks Pipkins' return to the public eye after a long legal battle with the actor who played his grandfather, over sordid allegations involving drugged toffees.

JANE STENCH (Fanny)
Jane Stench won an Olympic Gold medal for figure skating aged sixteen. During a long struggle with alcohol she launched an innovative show combining ice dance with Irish dance and acrobatics, which was sadly forced to close after a series of bloody accidents. 'Bobo' marks her debut on a West End Stage not covered with ice.

BARRY WILMOT (Sniper Hawkins)
Barry Wilmot is a versatile actor/writer who began his career starring in Andrew Lloyd Webber's roller-skating Turkish prison drama 'Midnight Express'. He has also worked extensively with Shirley Conran, most notably adapting her popular series of 'Lace' novels for the stage, as 'Which One Of You Bitches is my Mother'.

SPECIAL NOTICE
Please keep all aisles clear during the performance. Would those seated in the Upper Circle rows W to Z please be ready to catch Mr. Hoskins at the climax of the 'Human Cannonball' number.

THE 'SONG FOR BOB HOSKINS' SING-ALONG!

Tickle me fancy,	Rattle me spoonies,	Polish me pearlies,	Long me Good Friday
Av a banana,	Nibble me knob,	Apples and pairs,	Ragged me Rawney,
What a palava,	Shiver me timbers,	Buckets' o' fun,	Roger me Rabbit,
Old bull and bush!	Corn on the cob!	And a barrel o' laughs!	Mona me Lisa!
Apples and pears,	Shuffle me bobkins,	Naughty old Nancy,	Cockle me coppers,
Scruffle me nuts,	Tackle me tits,	Slappin' her knees,	Twizzle me stick,
I'm off to Stepney,	Toddy me pipkins,	Saucy aunt Sally,	Spank me behind,
To waggle me brush!	Fiddle me nips!	Jellied me eels!	For just two and six!

2 Why not use one of the hundreds of festering old bottles of 'Revitalising Bath Gelee' that your aunt's been giving you for Christmas for the last ten years? You know it'll just make the water all polluted and slimy but you've got to get rid of that crap somehow.

3 If you expect your bath to take ages to fill, it will do so in seconds, and vice versa. It's best to leave it running and go and commence your preliminary fashion preparations in another room, then dash back to check it every thirty seconds.

4 Do not use bubble bath. The whole concept is a myth perpetuated by actors in adverts and movies who don't want to show their bits. No commercially available bubble-bath will be as frothy and satisfying as it looks on the telly, and no amount of water churning will make the ensuing froth last for more than ten seconds.

It's Friday night. You're back from work and have only half an hour before you're due on a hot date. Your private areas need cleaning, just in case you're fortunate enough to provoke some kind of intrusion into your pants. You could take a shower, but for some unfathomable reason, you decide to treat yourself to a bath. Up your chances of a trouble free wallow by following these simple steps.

1 Set the hot and cold taps at your estimated optimum output level. But don't worry about it too much, because whatever you do will fail. By the time you come back, your bath will always be too hot or too cold or too full or too empty.

A&J'S GUIDE TO
BATH

5 Do not attempt to use any other taps in the house while running a bath. Your plumbing system was invented by Wilf Lunn and installed by The Chuckle Brothers long before you moved in, and as such can only supply one tap in one room at any one time.

6 When your bath is full, you'll inevitably find that it's much too hot or too cold, and you'll have to drain some water out. To do so you'll need to perform the painful Zen Plug Grab ritual. This requires total concentration and must be executed with one high-speed precision manoeuvre. If you miss the plug with your first plunge your arm will be badly scalded and you will need hospital.

7 So far you have been testing the temperature with your arm, whose nerves are now so scalded and confused that they no longer give a true reading. So when you finally strip off and lower

your naked body in... Ow! Ow! Owww! It hurts! You'll crouch in the water for a moment, thinking you'll get used to it. The smell of your nether regions will drift up as if pleading to be washed, but it's just too hot. Terrified that your feet will be melted right off, you'll soon leap out again.

8 Now you're standing alone in the bathroom, naked, shivering and confused. Your skin is bright red and may well be peeling off. You have instantly developed the veins of an eighty year old. Before you sits a tub of scummy water about as inviting as an acid bath. You've got five minutes left before you're due to leave. So just take a shower will you?

TRAUMA

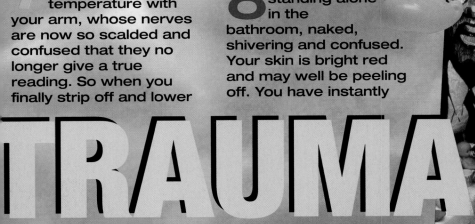

A&J's Guide to Record Stores

STATISTICS THAT I'M just about to make up say that young people spend over seventy per cent of their lives in record shops. To make sure this time is spent as happily and productively as possible, follow our simple colour coded guide.

▼ The Specialist Dance Outlet

The most frightening of all record shops, often found on fashionable side-streets, surrounded by smaller, equally intimidating designer clothes shops. Throbbing beats from within should be audible several streets away.

There's a gang of frightening looking hip-hop goons in stupid hats hanging out in the doorway. Don't be afraid, anyone who spends all day posing outside record shops has to be a wussy. Just push past.

It's more like a private nightclub than a shop inside. There's no sales assistant, just a DJ. No-one seems to

be buying anything, just nodding along to the deafening beats. Buy some time browsing, and nod along too. You will be slowly registered as 'okay' by everyone else.

Chances are you won't know the exact name of the record you want, as you've only half heard it on the radio. On no account attempt to sing it to the sales staff, as you will look and sound like an arse.

If in doubt, point at a random cool-looking sleeve, then ask for two just to make it look like you know what you're doing. It's worth paying ten pounds just to get out with your reputation intact.

★ Display Racks
Stay away from hands-on display racks on the shop floor. These never contain anything worth buying, all the good stuff's always behind the counter. Looking at them only broadcasts the fact that you're an amateur.

★ Counter
To get to the counter, use the same technique as you would getting to the bar in a packed pub. Shove gently, brandish money, and try to claim a place on the counter with your hand as soon as possible.

★ Club Flyers
On your way out, do not look at or pick up any of the club flyers stacked by the door. Doing so only advertises the desperate state of your social life.

★ CDs
On no account ask for anything on CD, or you'll be told to piss off back to Our Price where you belong.

Key to Floorplan

- ■ Obscure imports
- ■ Intimidating musos
- ■ Dodgy club flyers
- ■ 50 gigawatt speakers
- ■ Boyish smell
- ■ Very very baggy trousers
- ■ Sticky floor
- ■ Random threats

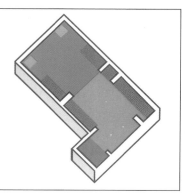

▶ The Record and Tape Exchange

Commonly found in market streets between a hippy craft shop and butcher's, these are basically just pawn shops for people with no possessions of any value.

You're here on business, so you'll want to go straight to the counter with your stack of sacrificial records. Remember, you've entered a world where what you think makes an album valuable means nothing.

Expect extreme surliness from the counter staff, as they flick disdainfully through your offering. It's not just your collection they're valuing, it's your personality, and it doesn't look good.

When the valuation comes, prepare for a hard slap in the face. When they say 'ten cash', they mean pence, not pounds. Don't bother arguing. Try not to cry.

Key to Floorplan
- Unlikely rarities
- Desperate alcoholics
- Surly staff
- Unutterable rubbish
- Disillusioned punters
- Piles of rotten fruit

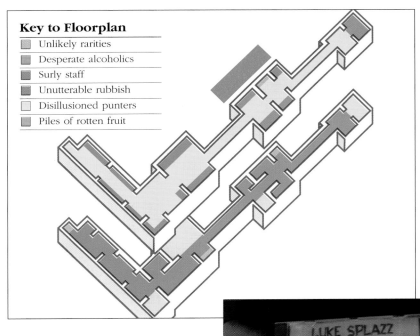

Next they'll offer you an alternative 'exchange' value, often more than double the cash value. Suddenly feeling like a kid in a candy store, you'll accept.

Only as you excitedly browse the racks will the truth slowly sink in. This shop is stocked entirely with shite.

★ Rare Displays
Do not be impressed by the super-rare albums up on the walls. They are purely for decoration, nothing like them has ever been bought or sold here.

Every artist or band is represented only by their worst work. You came to get rid of crap records, and now you're gonna leave with twice as many even crapper ones.

▶ The Record Megastore

Walk down any high street in the world and pretty soon you'll find an unfeasibly large record megastore, usually between McDonald's and WH Smith.

On entering, take a deep breath and thank Jesus that places like this exist. Giant record shops are one of the greatest achievements of the late twentieth century.

Be informed and entertained by the in-store DJ as he serves up a tasty mix of music and bullshit. But never buy anything he plays. Records that sound amazing the first time always turn out to be no good.

Enjoy the heady dizziness as you twist and turn down hundreds of aisles, desperately trying to find the right letter in the right section. These stores are confusingly laid out on purpose, to make customers light-headed.

When you do find the section

you're looking for, be careful not to disturb the smelly slacker who'll almost certainly be draped over it, endlessly rifling.

Instead of the CD you wanted, you'll most likely find a stack of empty section cards. Take a moment to marvel at how such a vast shop can so persistently fail to have what you want. Now make some impulse purchases to cheer yourself up.

★ Listening Posts
Avoid listening posts, they are weird, they make you look like a prat and they pump subliminal messages into your brain.

★ Classical Section
If the crowds and in-store music get too much, head for the chill-out zone that is the classical

department. Use the deserted cash desk to pay for your dangerous, non-classical purchases.

★ Refund Desk
When you bring a CD back for a refund and they ask you what's wrong with it, never tell the truth. Always use the following lie:"I bought it for my friend's birthday,

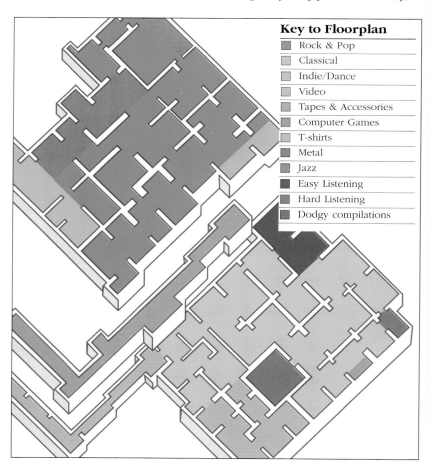

Key to Floorplan	
■	Rock & Pop
■	Classical
■	Indie/Dance
■	Video
■	Tapes & Accessories
■	Computer Games
■	T-shirts
■	Metal
■	Jazz
■	Easy Listening
■	Hard Listening
■	Dodgy compilations

IF MOVIES REALLY WERE JUST LIKE VIDEO GAMES

Everybody keeps telling us that modern movies are becoming more and more like video games. If that were really true, this is what we'd be watching...

The Matrix: The world would quickly clue into the fact that reality is a computer generated simulation, when they notice that people's limbs stick through solid walls unaccountably.

Tron: Instead of racing light-cycles and duelling with iridescent frisbees, the people inside the computer would spend all their time playing Blackjack and searching for porn.

Psycho: Instead of dying in the shower scene, Janet Leigh would have three more lives left. On her second try she'd knee him in the nuts and get on with her life.

Independence Day: The story would stop every five minutes and audiences would have to sit and stare at a 'loading' screen. Or Bill Pullman acting. Same thing really.

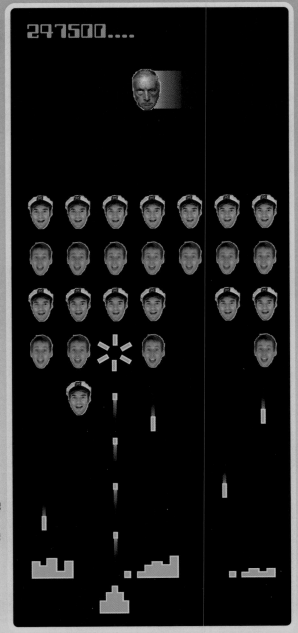

247500....

Die Hard: Bruce Willis would have to wear a head-to-toe suit of large cardboard boxes painted with clothes and a bad likeness of his face.

Rambo: John Rambo would kill hundreds of Vietcong by jumping on their heads and collecting a piece of fruit from each one.

Day of the Jackal: Edward Fox would find a cheat code to give De Gaulle a huge head, making his sniping much simpler.

Star Wars: Just as Luke prepares to fire the fateful shot into the Death Star's reactors, he'd run out of fifty pence pieces and have to fly back to the cantina for change.

Four Weddings and a Funeral: Sonic the hedgehog would be the best man, and instead of forgetting the ring, he'd have hundreds of the bastards.

Dr Fischer Verlag's
Encyclopedia Of Partial Medicine

PART TWO: WANKING

Stand up and let your arms swing loose and you will see the most natural place for your hands to be is next to your joolies. Masturbation, autoeroticism, onanism, call it what you will; I prefer to use the correct medical term: WANKING. It is a scientific fact that all men wank. Your boss wanks, your teachers wank, your Dad wanks and you wank, assuming you're a man that is. And even if you're a woman, you probably wank too (though you often don't admit it.)

However, despite the fact that men spend an average of 15 weeks a year wanking*, there is a paucity of information available on the subject to help the novice or the curious wanker. Here then, are some important medical facts about the most fun a man can have on his own. To avoid becoming over-excited I will confine my observations to my fellow male wankers.

WHAT CAN I WANK OVER?

PORN

Pornography, some say, has been the driving force behind every significant technological innovation of the 20th century. When you buy a new camera, a new video machine, or a new computer it's really only a matter of time before you begin to realise the potential these items have for helping you wank. Porn is a fun short cut but excessive use could make you lazy and jaded. Why not try these other less exploitative sources...

FILTHY THOUGHTS

Use your brain to recall great sexual encounters from the past, or imagine new liaisons with a vast array of people. But be warned! There is no legislating for the guests that can appear, often uninvited in the feverish mind of a wanker. There's your cousin! The old dinner lady! Your best friend's Mum! *Your* Mum! Does this make you a sick, perverted serial killer? Only if you go on sick, perverted killing sprees afterwards.

'NON PORNOGRAPHIC' PRINTED MATERIAL

Lingerie catalogues, advertisements for breast enlargement clinics, fashion spreads in The Face, and the instructions from a packet of tampons. All of them have done the trick at one time or another.

WHERE CAN I WANK?

The wonderful thing about wanking is you can do it anywhere you like though some locations tend to be a little more practical, as long as you are observing the correct procedures.

IN BED

Lying there in total comfort, one can sometimes feel overwhelmed by the temptation to enjoy a quick wank. There is nothing wrong with this as long as you have one of the following items handy: A tissue. A sock. A hand. A pants. A sponge. Failure to use the items is squalid and non-hygienic.

ON THE LAV

Ah the lav. Lockable haven, convenient in every way, except for the lack of a table for reading material. I am in the process of designing a toilet seat that comes with a kind of school desk attachment to solve this very problem. It will be called The Lavatreat.

IN THE BATH

A bath wank has the disadvantages of being noisy and a little disgusting at the end, but sometimes, you have to do it. Please rinse the tub thoroughly when you have finished your wank, it may be my turn to use the bath.

*I may have invented this statistic from nowhere.

IS THERE JUST THE ONE TECHNIQUE?

Indeed no, my wanky friend! The most conventional method is what doctors call 'The Five Knuckle Shuffle'. Up and down, up and down, varying the speed and the grip as you like (or as you seldom like if someone is doing it to you). But there are other ways...

UNFAMILIAR HAND

This is fun if you're at a loose end. Either use the hand you do not normally use, or sit on your regular hand until it is numb. It feels a little like someone else has joined you! You can also try dipping your hand in hot water for a minute or so for an momentary thrill bonus.

THE ROLLING PIN

Keeping your palms open, get a rolling action going as if you were making a plasticene snake at school. You'll be surprised how quickly you reach the end of your journey, which is ideal for the busy modern man.

THE NOOGIE

Using one hand to grip, roll the palm of the other across the top, fairly fast. This can be painful if done improperly, so do be careful.

THE LUCKY PILLOW

No hands. Just a pillow. This is a favourite with younger men and does tend to be rather labour intensive. Not recommended if you're staying at a friends house. Unless you do not like the friend. Or you like them a great deal.

SOME MYTHS DISPELLED

As a young man, I was assured by my classmate Karim Fadli that every man has only a finite number of ejaculations in him. I resolved to put this theory to the test by wanking more than is necessarily normal. That was many years ago, and I am pleased to say the theory appears to be bogus, though I will of course continue with the experiment to be thorough.

Other myths are that wanking can lead to blindness, psychosis, eternal damnation and depression. I have not found any of these to be true. I am lucky enough to be happy, healthy, wealthy and something of a genius, and I believe it is all thanks, to my many wanks.

HOW MUCH IS TOO MUCH?

When you start missing appointments and lose touch with your friends, that may be too much. Also when you are arrested for wanking on the bus. That is almost certainly too much. However if you don't get caught, you're sorted.

A&J'S boring meal survival guide

All of us have to endure tedious meals out with boring friends or relatives once in a while. From the moment you sit down, you want to leave, and the supposedly enjoyable rituals of eating quickly become torture. The only way to survive is to make full use of the many fiddling opportunities around you.

Candle fiddles

(a) Snap off big dry drips of wax and melt them in the flame.

(b) Press the top edges of the candle inwards and watch as hot wax builds up then gradually overflows.

flame pain endurance test. Intense pain may help you forget the tedium around you.

(c) Use a match to create little notches in the side of the candle, and watch as hot wax cascades through them satisfyingly.

(d) Dip your fingertips into the hot wax, let them dry, then tap them together for rewarding inter-finger tactility.

(e) Peel some soft wax from the candle and mould it into strange, anxious ,sculptures. Allow to dry and create a small table-top art exhibition.

(f) Finally, try the finger-in-the-

Table-cloth fiddles

(a) Make multiple vertical tears in the edge for an attractive fringe effect. Do this just above your knees and it'll be your special secret Hawaiian hula-skirt.

(b) Make similar tears, but now roll each section up tightly and unfurl at different lengths to make an attractive bouncy-curled fringe to play with.

(d) Rip a long strip off, fold in a concertina, and tear a little person shape with the arms and feet linking at the sides. Unfold to create a row of

tragic little people.

Fag packet fiddles

(a) Pull the plastic wrapping halfway off the packet, then fold it up neatly around the base. Now pull it back up and watch your neat folds unfurl and re-take their shape magically.

(b) Again with the plastic half off, see if you can stand the

packet up so it appears to be 'floating' above the table on the flimsy cellophane support. Now tap it and watch it the box slide back into its wrapper.

(c) This time, remove the cellophane entirely and try and slip it back on the opposite end. This exercise might drive you insane, but it's worth it when you succeed.

(d) Now half remove the cellophane again. Using a lit butt, burn a single hole in the centre. Now blow smoke inside and tap the wrapper to create smoke rings.

(e) Balance the packet half off the edge of the table, flip it up in the air with a downward swipe of your hand and try to catch it in mid-air.

Beer bottle fiddles

(a) If the label is moist, drag your fingernail down it repeatedly, and it should softly and satisfyingly crumple in strips.

(b) If the label is very damp and loose, try pushing it around to hilariously 'wrong' positions on the bottle.

(c) If the label is dry, try ripping it off completely without damaging or tearing it. If you manage the above, roll it up tightly and pop it between your lips like a cigarette for everyone to admire.

Food fiddles

(a) Boredom is bad for the appetite, so it's more than likely you'll have to conceal some unwanted food. Avoid embarrassment and have fun at the same time by seeing how much food you can compact into one corner of your plate.

(b) Another good way to get rid of unwanted food is to loudly declare how delicious it is then offer it around for sampling. Before you know it your companions will have consumed half your disgusting meal for you.

(c) Try arranging your food artistically. Make a portrait of the person sitting opposite you. If things are getting really desperate, try forming the words 'HELP ME' out of carrots.

Ice fiddles

(a) If your drink is graced with cylindrical ice cubes, try and thread as many as you can on your straw. Now attempt to remove it without any ice slipping off.

(b) If your drink is crammed with ice cubes, use the tip of your straw to repeatedly dunk them under the surface.

Coaster fiddles

(a) Cardboard coasters are great for ripping apart. See how many thin paper layers you can separate before the thing disintegrates.

(b) If your coaster is very damp, fold the exposed edges of the coaster up around the base of your glass to create a mini coaster-cup for your glass

Ashtray fiddles

(a) Every time you stub out a cigarette, use the butt to push all the filth in the ashtray to one side, and polish the glass bottom until it's totally clean.

(b) This time, push all the butts to one side but leave ash covering the base. Now draw a picture in the ash. The only limit is your imagination!

(c) If you have a box of matches to hand, try impaling your used fag butts on individual match-sticks, like foul little cocktail sausages. Offer them around to your mates as a satirical snack.

ROBERT DE NIRO CALYPSO

Chorus:
His name is .Bobby, oooh
Bobby De Niro, aaah
He's a loverly pers-juan, oooh
And a very good actor, aaah

Once upon a time in America
Huston Huston Huston Huston Angelica
He's a super actor and a very lovely guy
With a cheeky smile and a mole under
one eye

Chorus

He was in Godfather 2 but not
Godfather 3
Are you, are you, are you looking at me
He could teach Kevin Bacon a thing
or two
Looking, looking, looking at me are you?

Chorus

He played Jake La Motta in the film of
'Raging Bull'
He ate, he ate, he ate, he ate til he was
full
He tried some comedy in a film with
Seany Penn
He will never never never do that again

Chorus

But when he is not acting
People say he is <u>boring</u>
But I do not believe them
It is you that is <u>boring</u>

In 'Midnight Run' he showed to us a
lighter acting style
Proving he could swear a lot but also
make you smile

This world is full of bad men but Bobby
still repeats
Some day a rain will come and wash the
scum off all the streets

Chorus x 2 ...FLASH!

LOUISE'S PAGE

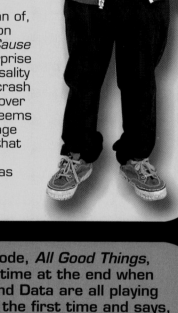

**Hello, my name is Louise
This is my Louise page
Read it please
I liked Enemy Of The State
And anything with Will
Smith, he is great.**

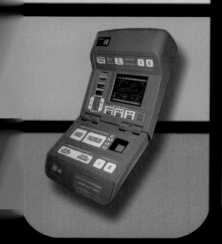

I am number 1 fan of a lot of things, which you might think you like too, but I doubt you like them as much as me. I'm the number 1 fan of: The X Files, Ben Folds Five, Final Fantasy and Tomb Raider for Playstation, Solero balls, Barenaked Ladies, ER, Friends, Cool hats, Will Smith, Dawson's Creek, Frasier, Kelly Brook and Countdown.

But of all things I am the number 1 fan of, the best is Star Trek The Next Generation (or TNG). My favourite ever episode is *Cause and Effect* (season 4) in which the Enterprise is caught in a temporal anomaly (or causality loop) that makes them play poker then crash into another ship and blow up over and over again! It's like five episodes in one and seems to go on for ages. At the end they manage to avoid the other ship and it turns out that Frasier is the captain, so it's the best episode of anything ever made, and it was directed by Jonathan Frakes who plays Commander Riker, the beardy one.

I watched the final feature length episode, *All Good Things*, 28 times in one week and cried every time at the end when Worf, Beverly, Deana, Geordi, Riker and Data are all playing poker and Jean Luc Picard joins in for the first time and says, "I should have done this a long time ago." I am crying now, just thinking about it.

Apart from *Cause and Effect*, I like any episode that has the Borg in it. I love the Borg because they don't try to show off and be funny at parties, they just assimilate people. I wish I was Borg because I would be part of the collective and people wouldn't ignore me and I could get served quicker in pubs. I would have a telly in my stomach and a playstation in my trousers. Also when girls told me to piss off I could just say 'RESISTANCE IS FUTILE' and assimilate them.

TNG I LOVE YOU

TO THE CAST OF TNG.
YOU KILLED
MY SHOW
NOW I WILL
KILL YOU
louise

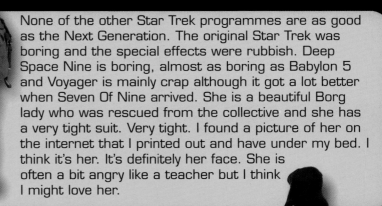

The worst day of my life was when TNG finished. At first I was very angry and wrote a letter to the cast threatening to kill them if they didn't make any new episodes. I didn't mean it, but the police called my house and told me never to write again. It was frightening but it taught me a lesson. Now I don't put my address and phone number on my letters.

None of the other Star Trek programmes are as good as the Next Generation. The original Star Trek was boring and the special effects were rubbish. Deep Space Nine is boring, almost as boring as Babylon 5 and Voyager is mainly crap although it got a lot better when Seven Of Nine arrived. She is a beautiful Borg lady who was rescued from the collective and she has a very tight suit. Very tight. I found a picture of her on the internet that I printed out and have under my bed. I think it's her. It's definitely her face. She is often a bit angry like a teacher but I think I might love her.

THE STAR TREK SONG

Star Trek, The Next Generation
You're loved throughout the
    nation,
You're my favourite show!
(I've seen every episode)

You're lucky!
You don't have to wait for buses!
You just step into the
    transporter...
        And off you boldly go.

Mr Worf's my
favourite person
Because he's very
strong and large.
Jean Luc Picard is
fair but hard,
He has to be 'cos he's
in charge.

When I found out
    that it was ending
I wrote them all a
    letter
To say they had to die.
(They sent policemen round
    to see me)

Now my whole life is
    rather empty
Because you've gone and
    left me

Where did you boldly go?
Where did you boldly go?!
Where did you boldly go?!
WHERE DID YOU BOLDLY GO?

I think about Worf, Jean Luc, Data and Geordi, (but not Deana and Beverly so much) every day. Watching repeats is OK, but it's like being on the holo-deck with the safety protocols on, it doesn't feel as exciting as a new episode. I miss them so much and I wish it never finished. I can't wait for the new TNG film, but it won't be the same. Why does everything have to change?

Everyone loves to get something for nothing, and there's no easier way to do exactly that than to borrow stuff from your mates. But borrowing can also lead to shattered relationships and treasured possessions being lost forever. Be forewarned and forearmed with Adam & Joe's guide to lending protocol.

LENDING TO CLOSE FRIENDS
Everyone likes to lend things to close friends. It's the kind of activity that cements relationships, giving both parties a warm glow of mutual trust.

Months later you'll feel the urge to use the item and soon you'll be on the phone asking for it back.

The close friend will blithely promise to bring it the next time they see you.

SECONDARY LENDING
Secondary lending is when someone borrows something from you then lends it to someone else. If you're lucky, the initial borrower will ask your permission, but this is very unusual.

LENDING TO NEW FRIENDS
Lending to new friends is an even more attractive proposition. There's no better way for you to demonstrate what a nice person you are, and for them to show that they want to see you again.

Months later you'll feel the urge to use the lent item.

Of course, they'll forget. You'll feel unable to bully them about it because you don't want to seem like a tight git.

Of course, the initial lending was so long ago you can't be totally sure that they're lying. What usually happens next is a huge pathetic fight.

Months later you'll feel the urge to use the lent item.

If there are two people between you and your precious belonging, the only way to retrieve it is to launch a sustained campaign of pedantic phone calls and gratuitous social visits.

When you claim it be your own, they deny ever borrowin it. Often they'll clair that they gave you back your copy and bought their own.

You realise that not only have you had no contact with the supposed new friend since that first visit, but you don't even have their number.

In doing so you'll make two people think you're a tight git and damage your reputation doubly.

Whatever it is you lent them, you can kiss it goodbye. In the long run it's better to value friendship above material possessions, you tight git.

So you've lent various books, CDs and videos to old and new friends, never to see them again. Months later you're round at one of these friends' houses and you spot something you lent them sitting innocently on their shelf.

Even if you get the number, you can't possibly call them up just to hassle them about it, because they'll think you care more about the lent item that you do about seeing them again.

A&J PRODUCTS – IDEAL FOR LENDING!

(you'll never see them again and you won't care!)

ADAM & JOE FEATURING ZAC
THE FOOTIE SONG

F.U.R.E.N.D.S

COURTENEY COUTS & CO   MATHEW PERRY PERRY RICH   MONEVFER OLDROPE   MATT LE BANK   LEASE A CLONDO WINN   DAVID SWINDLER

THE ONE WITH THE SHITTY OLD TOYS IN IT

THINK V.D.

Monday 17th April 18st 13, cakes 9 (cake good), pies 20 (pies v v good), calories 897760 (not bad for the amount of cakes and pies) positive thoughts not related to cakes and pies 0 (vg)

.59 pm

'Hellen Fiddling is the best writer in the world and Piglet Jones is the best book in the world'
Nick Football

Piglet Jones's diary
Hellen Fiddling

BOLLOCKBUSTERS

FREE cut-out-and-keep

BOWIE MOVIE MARATHON

by KENNETH KORDA

Into the Night/ 1986

Quintessential Jones. "Oh you're good, you're very good," he keeps saying to Jeff Goldblum, because he thinks he's a killer like him you see. He's not though, he's just a normal up guy swept along by a chain of bizarre events like in *After Hours* with Martin Short. Does not sing.

Jesus of Nazareth/ 1932

David plays Pontius Pilate. "I wash my hands of this," he says. Again no songs.

Underground/ 1976

Especially good as his scrotum is clearly defined through his pixie king leggings. Sings several above-average songs and acts beautifully with the muppets. (For proper view of winkle see *The Man Who Fell To Earth*.)

Absolute Beginners/ 1980
Jazzin' for Blue Jean / 1978

David Bowie shines in these seminal British movies both directed by Bob Hoskins. Also sings constantly throughout managing to upstage Smiley Culture on the extended soundtrack album by a short way. His version of 'Volare' is not as good as 'That's Motivation!' which is my favourite Bowie song. If I could I would cast him as Danny Wahlberg in my forthcoming New Kids On The Block movie.

Freejack/ 1996

"Get the meat!" he snarls from his tank in this vision of the future gone horribly wrong. Stepped in when Mick Jagger pulled out because of lumbago and does a bang up job, managing to look and sound just like Mick. "Get the meat!" Marvellous. Bye now!

Introduction
by Jeremy Beadle

It's perhaps fitting that I write this intro-
duction in telly jail - that graduate school of
great television pranksters. If it is a crime
to subvert public notions of obedience, to
dissect the intrinsic tissues of artifice, to
swap a bloke's car with an identical one then
push it off a cliff, then dig it - I am guilty.
In TV prison we gather round the capitalist
brainwash box that is television and breathe
the anarchist oxygen of Adam and Joe's pranks.
Their names join the illustrious roster of
revolutionary artists who
have struggled to liberate
us from the sterile
machines of corporate
death. Great artists like
Duchamp, Abbie Hoffman,
William S. Borroughs, Boyd
Rice, Timothy Leary, Henry
Kelly, Mandy Dingle, Dennis
Norden, Noel Edmonds, Cilla
Black and that bloke off
Candid Camera. And so
I urge you young
cats to steal these
pranks. They are a
manual for survival
in the prison that
is Britain. And
remember - free
speech is the
right to shout
'theatre!' in a
crowded fire.

Jeremy Beadle
December 1970, Cook
County Telly Jail,
Chicago.

**TWENTY PERCENT
FREE**
Go into a grocery
store and find
products with a free-percentage
special offer. Now eat/drink/pocket that per-
centage of the contents. If anyone tries to
stop you, just say 'but it says it's free!' over
and over again to whatever
they say.

**DOMESTIC MAKEOVER
SHOW**
Pose as a TV crew
and convince
someone to let you
make over a room
in their house in
their absence.
Come up with a
ridiculously over-
ambitious concept, use cheap crap as materials
and only your most cack-handed decoration
skills. Reveal the new room to your victim and
film their anguished reaction. Remember, the
'Changing Rooms' team never repair what they've
done, so neither should you.

**YOU BREAK IT,
YOU PAY FOR IT**
Find a fragile goods
shop with a sign
saying 'you break it,
you pay for it'.
Bring a hammer and a
wad of cash and start
smashing things. When
they confront you,
say 'well I wanted to
just buy it, but the sign
says...'. Give them cash for what you've
smashed and carry on breaking and paying.

THESE PRANKS!

HUSTLING COMPETITION
With a friend, locate your nearest hustling area and take it in turns to strut your sweet asses. When a car pulls up, approach the window and offer to run your fingers through their hair for £250, or kiss them on the cheek for £500. They'll

soon lose interest and bugger off, and the one who pulls the most punters wins.

PAVEMENT PORTRAIT ARTIST
All you need to be one are some professional drawings of celebrities to draw the punters in. Begin the best portrait you're capable of, then slowly give in to your laziness and let it go shit. Enjoy as your innocent sitter reads the confused reactions of their watching friends. Then reveal the full crapulous horror of your finished work and don't let them leave without paying.

MIME IS MONEY
Go to a public area dressed as Marcel Marceau, Charlie Chaplain, a robot or a Greek statue. You now have a licence to annoy strangers with your skill-free mime, then demand they pay you to go away. Lazier mimes can just stand very still with an upturned hat at their feet. When someone puts money in, move a tiny bit. The kids love it.

PISS UP IN A BREWERY
Fill a van with mates, booze, party hats and balloons, then drive to your nearest brewery and see if you can organise a piss up there. Security guards, receptionists and senior staff will try to block your entry, so head for the goods yard, where the workers won't care enough to stop you. See how much of a piss-up you can have before you're thrown out, and never let anyone accuse you of not being able to organise one again.

⏸ ⏩ VINYL JUSTICE DEPARTMENT: ⏪ ⏸
TOP TEN ALBUMS OF ALL TIME, DEFINITELY, EVER

Good afternoon. It won't have escaped your attention that a new list of the all-time best albums ever is published every 20-30 seconds in one of the music periodicals. These tend to feature the usual suspects over and over with a token few current titles that probably won't make another list again (unless it's a 'most boring albums of all time' list). So we here at the Vinyl Justice Department have decided to clear up any confusion by publishing the definitive all-time top 10 best albums ever made which will serve as the industry standard from here on.

HOW WE ARRIVED AT THE FINAL LIST

That is a fascinating question and we are very glad you asked it, young ladyman. We fed the results of every best album poll into our Musox mainframe database unit and switched it off. Then we got out our favourite albums and wrote down the titles. The rest is music history...

WHAT MAKES A GREAT ALBUM?

Another pertinent if rather cheeky question. Of course talking in absolute terms about the quality of music is meaningless because the enjoyment of all art is by nature entirely subjective, but there are a few things we can be quite certain of:
A GREAT ALBUM...
1. Must have been made in the eighties.
2. Must contain at least one or more hit singles.
3. Must have a really cool cover.
4. Should have a David Bowie connection.

10. THE HOUSEMARTINS: LONDON 0 HULL 4

Marred only by some superfluous political posturing, the Housemartins' debut is a veritable trove of musical nuggets that The Beautiful South could only dream of approximating. The single 'Happy Hour' had a funny video which featured little clay versions of the band in a bar. At Happy Hour. The day Fatboy Slim left was the day his life turned to absolute shit. Like Pete Best leaving The Beatles, no amount of Zoe Ball can help you get over something like that.

9. DAVID BOWIE: NEVER LET ME DOWN

Conventional wisdom has it that Bowie reached his peak somewhere in the mid to late '70s but this album proves otherwise. A quick glance at the cover shows a man buzzing with madcap ideas for songs like 'Bang Bang' about guns, 'Glass Spiders' which deals with glass spiders, 'Zeroes', like 'Heroes' but with more Zzzzz and the single 'Day In Day Out' which was accompanied by a stunning video depicting the violent world of Los Angeles with two angels, one white and one black hovering above it all in an almost unbearably poignant one white, one black type way. Los Angeles. The Angels. Poignant.

8. GHOSTBUSTERS: ORIGINAL SOUNDTRACK

This album is superb on so many levels that our computer began to overheat and make funny clicking noises just trying to take them all in. A virtual Who's Who of rock, pop and boogie woogie, Ghostbusters features marvellous efforts from The Thompson Twins, Laura Branigan, The Bus Boys and of course, Ray Parker Jr whose single 'Ghostbusters' (with tune stolen from the equally superior Huey Lewis) is without doubt the best song ever written. It also features the best cover of all time.

7. LABYRINTH: ORIGINAL SOUNDTRACK

Not content with turning in a potentially Oscar-winning performance as the generously packeted Pixie King, Bowie once again ups the contemporary pop ante by coughing up the hit single 'Underground', possibly the other best song ever written. "It's only forever, not long at all..." he sings. Magnificent, because you see forever is a long

time, I mean it's forever really, so saying it's not long at all is er, crazy.

6. THOMPSON TWINS: QUICKSTEP & SIDEKICK

It's tough choosing just one great album by this combo but for sheer breadth and songs it has to be Quickstep. It's rammed with an embarrassment of classics like 'Watching', 'Love On Your Side', and of course 'We Are Detective' which employs Bailey's lyrical majesty to the fullest. "Woah oh, woah oh, woo woo ooh woo ho, woah oh, woah oh, woooooah ooh ooooh" he sings. Magic that only 2 Unlimited ever came close to recapturing.

5. CHART HITS 81:2

Most top 10s fail to give the proper respect to compilation albums. After all, if you take 20 of the best songs ever recorded and put them on one album, then it's going to be 20 times better than any other album isn't it? It's logic, that's all. Chart Hits was a classic of the genre but the one that re-wrote the compilation book was on the way...

4. RAIDERS OF THE POP CHARTS

Here we find Modern Romance, Raw Silk, Incantation, Tight Fit and Toni Basil to name but 5, all at their creative apex. To name but 4 more we also have Dave Stewart (not that one) and Barbara Gaskin (that one), Fat Larry's Band, Clannad, and The Chaps for whom great things still lie ahead. All this with a cover that boasts a very clever pastiche of a film that was popular at the time: Raiders Of The Lost Ark. By changing key words the designers have indicated that the artists featured on the record all

stormed or 'raided' the charts with their phenomenal pop skills. A man in a leather jacket with a whip, standing in a room with two potted palms in it further underlines the message that anyone purchasing the album can expect big-movie-style excitement. Part 2 also came free with part 1, making the whole package even more of a pop landmark.

3. DAVID BOWIE: TONIGHT

After the slight disappointment of 'Let's Dance', Tonight found Bowie refreshed, invigorated and right back on top of the pop heap with this remarkable collection of noise. Faced with the task of improving on Iggy Pop's song 'Tonight', Bowie drafts in Tina Turner to make the original sound like a lump of old shit. The same goes for his version of The Beach Boys' 'God Only Knows' which Bowie enhances with a very big orchestra and some wailing that evokes the real pain he must have been feeling for whatever reason. 'Dancing With The Big Boys' is also very very good.

2. NIK KERSHAW: THE RIDDLE

Perhaps the finest of all Kershaw's early eighties albums, The Riddle makes so called 'classics' by The Beatles, Led Zeppelin and Radiohead look like the tedious ramblings of stupid children. It's hard to believe that this one tape contains not only the title track, 'The Riddle', but 'Don Quixote', 'Wide Boy' AND 'Save The Whale'. Only Mike Tyson could provide so many devastating hits in such a short space of time and chew your ear off into the bargain.

1. ABSOLUTE BEGINNERS: ORIGINAL SOUNDTRACK

Never has the phrase 'original soundtrack' failed so completely to even hint at the kind of ground-breaking originality found on this recording. Absolute Beginners is the undisputed progenitor of Baggy, Britpop, Loungecore, Grebo and pretty much every significant musical movement since. Once again it's Bowie who dominates with the stirring saxophone epic 'Absolute Beginners', the unpredictable 'That's Motivation' and the definitive version of the Italian standard 'Volare'. That said, The Style Council, Smilie Culture, Tenpole Tudor, Working Week, Patsy Kensit and many many more all have a part in assuring this album a place at the very top of any serious 'best of' list.

YOU DANCIN'?

■ Enjoy going out to nightclubs but lack confidence in your dancing? Find that when you take to the dancefloor everyone else leaves? Get the feeling people are pointing and laughing at you? Help is at hand with these dancefloor survival tips ▶▶

YOU ASKIN'?

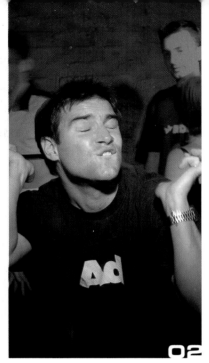

◀◀ 01 CHAIR DANCING

Chair Dancing is the low-effort, maximum-comfort alternative to standing-up dancing. It's ideal for people who feel the urge to dance but can't be arsed to stand up, and for those who know their seat will be stolen if they abandon it. Almost every upper-body move that you employ while standing-up dancing can be used when chair dancing, but do take care not to knock over nearby drinks.

◀ 02 THE WHITE MAN'S FUNK FACE

The dancer's face is the window to his soul, or his lack of it. When on the dancefloor, never clench your tongue between your teeth or bite your bottom lip. This is known as the 'White Man's Funk Face' and sends a direct message to other dancers that you are crap.

◀◀ 03 THE MONG

A better option is to wear a 'monged-out' expression. Let your mouth hang wide open, your eyes drop out of focus, and a small bead of dribble hang from your lower lip. Other dancers will think you're on impressively powerful drugs and excuse almost any level of poor dancing.

◀ 04 THE NON-COMMITAL NOD

A perennial favourite with those who like to stand at the edge of the dancefloor, but can't risk their cool by actually dancing. Simply hold a drink in one hand and a fag in the other and nod your head in time to the beat while staring patronisingly at other dancers. Do not do this for more than two or three tracks, as people will start to suspect the truth – you can't dance.

▲ 05 THE NUTTER

The opposite of the Non-Commital Nod is the Nutter. This dance requires zero skill but one hundred percent self-confidence. The idea is to dance incredibly badly with such violent energy that people are too afraid of you to laugh. Make sure to hold a beer bottle and wear an angry expression. When danced successfully, the Nutter should clear a wide radius around you.

▶ 06 THE HARMLESS PRAT

To dance the Harmless Prat you have to know you can't dance but just not care. This requires total un-selfconsciousness, a big silly grin on the face, and big silly dance moves. Make sure you look like you're having the time of your life and, instead of mocking you, people will admire your sheer joie-de-vivre.

▶ 07 THE BOOZE TRAIN

This is a great way to scratch your dance itch without actually committing to the dancefloor.

Position yourself on the opposite side from the bar, announce to your friends that you're going to get a drink, and set off across the middle of the dancefloor. Now make like a train, chugging along to the beat, nodding your head and pumping your fists back and forth. For a brief period you will actually be on the dancefloor dancing. But unlike other dancers, there is a purpose to your dancing. You have somewhere to go. You can speed up or slow down depending on how much you're enjoying yourself, or take an unnecessarily circuitous route through your fellow dancers. Remember to grin as you go, and people will think you're the life and soul of the party.

08

▲ 08 THE COPYCAT

This is perhaps the simplest of all survival techniques. Before you step out onto the dancefloor, scan your fellow dancers and target someone who is dancing modestly, but well. Now simply copy their moves. If they change their style to something too difficult or inappropriate, or if they spot you and move away, just fall into the Non-Commital-Nod until you see someone else to copy. There are drawbacks to this method, however. If too many people use it, before you know it the whole club is line-dancing, and must go home immediately.

▼ 09 THE OVER TWENTY-FIVES DISCO

If you are over twenty-five, there is a solution to all your problems: the over twenty-fives' disco. Just as *Just Seventeen* is read by thirteen-year-olds, so over twenty-fives discos are frequented by the over forties. In such company, the twenty-something dancer feels like a teenager again, safe in the knowledge that however badly they dance, the old codgers around them will think their hopeless moves are 'the latest thing'. If your younger friends think you're sad for going to these places, it should be easy to convince them that such clubs are the height of alternative fashion. After all, any club that doesn't let them in must be cool. ■

09

The sheer life-like brilliance of the fully animatronic waxworks at Dr. Spankle's will astound you! You'll feel like you've stepped right onto a Hollywood film set when you watch your favourite scenes from movie history happen right in front of you!

IF YOU'RE A THICK TOURIST, WHY NOT VISIT

DR SPANKLE'S
HOLLYWOOD
WAX-O-RAMA

'where the movies come alive before your eyes!'

WONK!

SEE! Tom Cruise's dangly bits in *Mission Impossible!*

SPLOTCH!

OH.

SEE! a dummy coming to life with Andrew McCarthy in *Mannequin!*

HURK!!

VONCE!

SEE! Al Pacino acts up a snowstorm!

SEE! Sharon Stone and Michael Douglarse in an unforgettably hairy moment from *Basic Instinct!*

WHAT?

88

■ 10% discount for Foreign Students in parties of over two hundred.

■ Visit Cafe Spankle: Wine and dine amongst genuine props and memorabilia from your favourite Hollywood movies, including one of Patsy Kensit's actual shoes from *Absolute Beginners*. Choose from three different flavours of potato crisp.

■ Visit Dr. Spankle's Souvenir-o-rama: *Mission Impossible* dangling Tom Cruise mobiles, limited edition Tom Hanks tubs of genuine *Philadelphia* Cream Cheese and a wide range of embroidered *Basic Instinct* sexy underwear.

■ Dr. Spankle's Wax-o-rama is open all day every day, and all night every night. Should Dr. Spankle's appear to be closed, please bang on doors firmly and persistently with both fists until a member of staff becomes available to assist you.

adam buxton
calls his ma

Valerie Buxton, 76, lives in Clapham with her rapper husband Nigel and her pot smoking son David. She thinks *Friends* is very well written and believes everything she reads in the *Daily Mail*.

Adam Buxton: *Hello, Ma?*

Valerie Buxton: I suppose you want picking up from the station. Nigel's taken the car for a drive-by and I don't know when he'll be back, so I'm afraid you're on your own.

AB: *Ma, it's Adam.*

VB: Adam! I thought you were David wanting a lift!

AB: *No it's me.*

VB: I was saying I couldn't have picked him up anyway because Nigel's taken the car.

AB: *So you said.*

VB: Adam! Great to hear from you! You sound just like David.

AB: *Right. Listen Ma, I don't know anyone famous so I was wondering if I could do the interview with you.*

VB: With Mel and Sue?

AB: *No, just with you. I'd better start .*

VB: Well, we ought to be quick because it's jolly expensive to call at this time.

AB: *But I phoned you.*

VB: Well, I don't know about that. We'll see.

AB: *What do you mean 'We'll see'?*

VB: What are you going to ask me? Nothing about Peter Mandelson. I can't stand him. Do you and your friends think he's cool? I can't see at all why people find him so funny. I think he's dreadful.

AB: *Don't worry about him. Here's my first question: Do you get better as you get older?*

VB: What a good question! Even when you were five or six you would ask the most perceptive questions. What is this or that. Everyone was always very impressed.

AB: *I think most six-year-olds ask those questions don't they?*

VB: Not like you.

AB: *Alright, but Ma, how about the question?*

VB: Must we talk about Peter Mandelson? I really think he is the bitter end.

AB: *Do you get better as you get older?*

VB: That's not quite such a good question. You have to come and see the new fridge! It finally arrived yesterday. Now we don't have to put everything in that frightful box.

AB: *Has it got a big freezer?*

VB: Frasier?

AB: *Freezer. You wanted a bigger freezer.*

VB: I like *Frasier*. It's very funny. It's very funny. The brother, what's he called?

AB: *Niles.*

VB: Neil. He's terribly good. I tried to watch your programme but I fell asleep.

AB: *Let's move on to the next question. Is it tough being a mum at the end of the 20th century?*

VB: Golly. Before I answer, have you written to your aunty Helen to thank her for your birthday cheque?

AB: *I haven't posted it yet.*

VB: Adam! It's been four months now! You must post it because I saw her last week and she mentioned that she hadn't heard from you again. Have you written to her?

AB: *No, but I will as soon as I've done this.*

VB: Please don't forget. What was the question?

AB: *It's okay, I've done them all now.*

VB: I think I hear Nigel. Do you want to speak to him?

AB: *I should go if I'm going to catch the post. Thanks Ma.*

VB: When are we going to see you?

AB: *I'd really better go. I think I see the postman.*

VB: Kevin Costner? I like Kevin Costner.

TOYTANIC
THE SMALL SCREENPLAY: PART 2

9. EXT: CROW'S NEST – NIGHT
WIDE of the front of the ship as it sails through the night, lights aglow. PUSH IN to the CROW'S NEST where two lazy mockney MICE sit with binoculars.

MOUSE 1: Lawd luvva duck! Iceberg, dead ahead!

MOUSE 2: Thank Gawd for that, I thought it'd never happen! Full speed ahead!

KEERRRUNCH! The ship hits the ICEBERG and begins to tip alarmingly. TOYS promenading on the deck start to SLIDE up and down.

TOYS: (Loving it) Wheeeeee! Yipeeeeee!

10. EXT: ELSEWHERE ON DECK – NIGHT
The ship's BAND are setting up.

LEADER: Okay boys, let's play something relaxing to calm everyone down.

MUSICIAN 1: What about 'Sailing' by Rod Stewart?

MUSICIAN 2: 'Shipbuilding' by Elvis Costello?

MUSICIAN 3: How about 'Underwater Love' from that jeans commercial?

LEADER: Nah, they're all totally inappropriate. Let's play 'Ship of Fools' by World Party.

11. EXT: BOAT – NIGHT
Crowds of toys are panicking on deck as ROSE confronts CAPTAIN JIM

ROSE: You heartless bastard! Those boats are half empty, and they're full of aquatic creatures!

CUT TO a boat containing only a jolly pink OCTOPUS.

OCTOPUS: (Posh) This is marvellous! So much more relaxing than swimming!

CAL pushes roughly through the crowds with a BABY ELEPHANT under his arm.

CAL: Out of the way! Let me through! This baby elephant's my son!

ELEPHANT: Huh! Don't flatter yourself you big rubber bastard!

The ELEPHANT wriggles free and flees.

12. EXT: ELSEWHERE ON DECK – NIGHT
CUT TO a BLACK AND WHITE shot of an sweet looking KENNETH MORE bear in a chunky roll-neck sweater and a sailor's hat.

KENNETH: Excuse me, I'm Kenneth More. I couldn't help noticing this is almost identical to my 1958 film A Night to Remember – apart from all your ridiculous made-up sub-plots and your crap script and acting.

CAL: (In colour) Shut up black-and-white boy! Nobody cares about you!

With that he PUNCHES KENNETH in his monotone mug.

13: INT: PIPE ROOM – NIGHT

JACK has been chained to a pipe, and ROSE wades towards him, axe in hand.

ROSE: I'll rescue you Jack!

JACK: Great, I always prefer to drown outdoors.

ROSE: Stay perfectly still, here goes!

She swings the axe down and – KERTHUNK! – it lodges firmly in JACK's skull.

JACK: (startled) Woah! Thank God I don't have a brain.

14. INT: STAIRWELL – NIGHT

ROSE and JACK are at the front of a crowd of third class passengers who crush desperately against iron gates which block their escape. A panicked STEWARD guards the gate with a gun.

JACK: Open this gate! We're all gonna die!!!

STEWARD: Stay back! It's trademarked and brand-name toys only!

JACK: You're gonna kill us just because we're handmade? Fascist bastard!

The crowd pushes down the gates and rushes out brandishing 80's hard left placards.

CROWD: Thatcher out! Class War! etc.

15. EXT: BOAT – NIGHT

TOYTANIC lurches forward in the water, then suddenly the centre of the boat SPLITS APART. JACK and ROSE are perched on the poop deck as it plummets down.

ROSE: Oh Jack! This is where we first met! Everything's come full circle!

JACK: Right, this whole thing's been a complete waste of everyone's time.

ROSE: I love you Jack. Nothing will ever come between us.

JACK: Er, did I mention I'm gay?

They edge forwards and kiss tenderly as the ship sinks into the sea.

16. EXT: SEA – NIGHT

ROSE floats on a large piece of wreckage, while JACK bobs beside her.

JACK: (dying) I can't hold on much longer Rose. . .

ROSE: (desperate) Don't go Jack! The film has to last more than three hours or we'll never get an Oscar. Jack. . . Jack. . . Jack!

JACK turns around to see NESSIE and the FROG sailing past happily.

NESSIE: (singing) Jack, jack, jack your body, jack jack jack your body!
JACK: Goodbye Rose!

JACK'S nose dips beneath the water and seconds later his head has disappeared too.

ROSE: Oh Jack, Jaaaack!

17. EXT: SALVAGE VESSEL DECK –

NIGHT

OLD ROSE on the deck, staring out to see wistfully, the MEDALLION in her hand.

OLD ROSE: Little did they know I had the medallion with me all the time!

Suddenly JIM'LL SAVILLE appears behind OLD ROSE and makes his trade-mark noise, which is impossible to spell.

JIM'LL: Ur-uh-ur-uh-ur-uh-ur! Now then now then guys'n'gals, what have we here then?

He's holding a viewer's letter which he reads out.

JIM'LL: Dear Jim'll, please could you fix it for me to see that stupid old woman from Toytanic returned to the ocean where she belongs. Yours hopefully, everyone in the world.

With that JIM'LL throws ROSE over the edge into the sea.

OLD ROSE: (plummeting) Waaaaaaaaaah!

JIM'LL: How's about that for a fixit then guys'n'gals?

Prime Time

BBC1	BBC2	ITV

BBC1

6.0 News Today
Something's happened! It's real. Possibly a fight, or a war, you just never know.

6.30 Regional News Ditch
A report the broken gas main that has been holding up traffic on Sleebitch Road.

7.0 I Am On A Free Holiday
Jane Slitt spends a week in a hotel and goes swimming. We see this.

7.30 Eastendtoys
Melvis has finally discovered Shaznay's secret, meanwhile Steve, Terry and Steve are shouting and pointing.

8.0 Aunty's Grody Pants
Cuddly old monster Terry Wogan unearths stones and dead relatives and laughs.

8.30 It's Lenny!
More sound and movement from Lenny Henry as he continues his life. Expect eight jokes.

9.0 The Launderette
Pat has a service wash to do before 5pm and Margaret has discovered someone using foreign coins in the powder dispenser.

Detective Spatchcock (Gary Kemp) is fresh on the trail of some hot lead (9.0pm)

9.30 Spatchcock
Spatchcock.

10.15 Foot Kick Ball Goal!
Sport quiz with Dan Cock and guests Charlie Coke, Norm Stick, Greg Repetitor and Bill Bald.

10.45 World Briefcase
Pat Bitch reports exclusively (not counting papers) from Purley where boys who like donkeys have refused to allow boys who like monkeys to eat Curly Wurlys or Toffo.

11.15 MOVIE
Shiney
(1997) Profoundly moving and talking true story of gifted tin Panda who plays the piano but loses his key after being wound up by his Dad too much. In real life it's not quite so funny and nice as it is in the film and he can't even play the piano that well, or that's what I heard anyway. Did you see that documentary about him? It was really interesting. It was on ages ago. Maybe they'll repeat it.

BBC2

6.0 Stuffed Trek: The Toy Generation
The Kindersurprise is caught in another temporal anomaly. Captain Pighard likes it, Lt Woof wants to attack it, Deana wants to understand it and Datoy doesn't have any feelings one way or the other.

6.45 Pop Slap!
Gurfin and Lilo from DirtyBoyz talk to Tina Frunt about their hair and nearly admit to being gay.

7.0 All Creatures Great And Cooked!
Ainsley Herriot fails to save the life of another sheep and eats it while laughing and laughing.

7.45 Room 2 Change
Pat Bitch and the team transform another perfectly normal room into a dirty dayglo plastic shitbox.

8.15 Badd Lucke
Terry Badd and Denny Lucke attempt to boost the ailing fortunes of their casino by hiring a stripper. Little do they know Dodgy Craig has a load of *paint* stripper to shift! Imagine the confusion! Terry and Denny will have to send it back and re-order! I just don't know.

A gravimetric tacheon burst from a phase inducer should cause a nanosingularity matrix.

9.0 Gardeners' Wildlife Cookup
Pippin Junkey rubs soil on his chest whilst eating grubs and voles, and Gertle Lechuga marks the 300th anniversary of the worm. Also Al Greenfinger shows you how to mend a broken artichoke.

10.0 Say Something Funny
Len Desk presides over another edition of the topical wake with guests Munty Cakes and Dan Cock.

10.30 Newdnight
Tetchy topical discussion conducted by the naked to spice it all up.

11.15 Art Basket
Mark Piskett is joined by Pepponet Shent, Kitty Foobash and Tommy Groin to cast a deliciously cocked eyebrow over the week's cultural phlegm. This week Carol Lichen's controversial 'My Pee Pee, Your Pee Pee' exhibition at the Infurion gallery and Dutch artist Lugort Meinhopper who eats his own feet whilst painting his arse.

ITV

6.0 Sarcastic News
The day's news given a sarcastic twist by Tim Dopper.

6.30 You Can Talk!
Viewers who have trouble with speaking, air their thought. Today, do banks discriminate against thieves?

7.0 Who Wants To Be Killed On Air?
Chris Tyrant fails to make anyone a millionaire but says "are you sure?" and "is that your final answer?" seventy eight times which is fun and exciting.

7.30 Larkfist Housing Area
Ricky can't understand why his second single hasn't risen more higher in the charts. Other things happen and it ends.

8.0 Blind Data
An in-depth look at the many ways you might die, focussing on people who are themselves about to expire.

8.30 When People Fall Over
Steve Shitt presents the same seven clips of people falling or slipping and talks between each one.

9.0 2 + 3 Makes Family Tree
It's the last in the series and Bostik is feeling guilty about shooting his family, with hilarious consequences!

Gloria Hunniford (Limahl) has had her fill of Steve (right) and plots. (4.0am)

9.30 Baddy Slappers
Sergeant Grist suspects Latoya of taking bribes off Stokesy and shouts at her in Cockney whilst drinking coffee. The camera is moving around very fast!
My friend Pete's in this one I think. He's the dead crack dealer.

10.0 News
News may not take place if nothing really important occurs.

10.30 MOVIE
Showtoys
(1997) A mucky poodle dreams of taking her clothes of on a stage with a fake volcano on it in this no-award-winning look at the world of swearing and toplessness directed by Paul Verbotten.

12.0 I'm Right, You're Wrong
Nick Hench watches more heated debate between 40 confused monkeys. This week, should string be shortened, and how touchable are tanks?

More Pish

CHANNEL 4

6.0 Dawson's Creepy Kids
Dawson's 4 year old son Musty is concerned that his friend Davina has been internalising her jelly-based rage issues while she is keen for Musty to face up to his gender conflicts and address his dummy envy. Both parts are played by thirty-year-olds in trendy nappies while some bad music plays.

7.0 Big News
A dull hour of recent nuts presented by several people sounding worried but excited.

8.0 Brookshite
Monica protests her innocence about shagging Ross's monkey while Joey insists he is from Liverpool.

8.30 Cooking Hurrah!
Monty Buggershop-Hooty prepares malted gay melon in chicken willy sauce for a group of very angry leprechauns.

9.0 Ally McSqueal
Ally & Biscuit take on a kooky case that is more complex than it first appears and win! Then Ally whines about being heartbroken and we actually see her heart break which is done with computer graphics!

Dog Ross has left to make a shit new film and Goose from Topgun is worried he can't leave.

10.0 EPR: Emergency Playroom
Decisions decisions. Doctors.

11.0 Naughty!
A visit to a room where everyone is nude! Plus an interview with someone nude! You can see her nipples! Also features the final of the Miss Nude Lady contest! Nude! Knockers!

NEW SERIES
11.30 Why Don't You Piss Off?
'In your face' comedy sketch show improvised live by Ben Fisst, Andy Graetch and Clare Spachula, winners of the Sunny Delight shouting and swearing award at the Edinburgh Whinge.

12.0 T.F.I. A Long Time Ago In A Galaxy far Far Away...
Repeated from last week and next week with guests Leia from the Alderandy Girls, Lager The Gutt and music from The Pet Shop Droids. Plus the return of Jar Jar Right, Jarr Jarr Left.

CHANNEL 5

6.0 Funny News
Serious news stories read by kids who keep giggling.

6.30 Dirty Birdies
The council wants to close the brothel but Mangie has a plan with some pairs of tits in it.

7.0 Not Making It
Another chance to laugh at the ambitions of young hopefuls. Look at them! Ha ha. Losers!

7.30 Cars And Trees
Clips of trees and cars. Tonight Poplar and Golf.

8.0 The Bob Frigg Show
The funnyman's off-the-wall tomfoolery wears a bit thin this week when he takes a shit on stage then wipes it onto his bald head.

9.0 Schindler's Guest List
Gail Porter and Noddy Holder join Liam Neeson for another mix of chat and grief.

10.0 Nina's Nipples
Nina sits and giggles while Andy tries to snog Mandy who starts to cry. Andy is so humiliated he becomes withdrawn and needs a course of therapy.

Blind Rock (10.45pm) not as good as watching another repeat of Furends on Sky 1 (12am–12pm)

MOVIE
10.45 Blind Rock
(1992) Made for TV drama about about a stone (or 'rock') born without ears, eyes or mouths who learns to suffer the ignorance of able-bodied people with dignity and even humour and music. Strong performances from Shirley Valentine and Jenny Powell make this about an hour and a half. Directed by Keith Chegwin.

12.15 Munty Cake's Sexy Yatter
Munty talks to Jineen Runtle about sex. 'Do you like big ones?' she asks them and they both laugh. Music from Carol Vorderman and Ricky Tickets plays his song.

1.0 European Punching, Kicking And Shoving
Coverage of European punching, kicking and shoving. Possibly nude.

2.0 Jedi Springer
'My Lover Is A Lying Pathetic Bastard!' Look at the crazy Yankees!

SKY ONE

6.0 Furends
The one where Ross becomes jealous when he finds an attractive bomb in Rachel's head.

6.30 Furends
The one where Joey loses his keys and has to impersonate Matthew Kelly to get them back.

7.0 The Simpsons
Rachel & Monica are mistaken for annoying rabbits and shot.

7.30 Furends
The one when Joey tries brain surgery, but he can't do it! Monica, Phoebe and Chandler laugh and laugh. Ross whines.

8.0 The X Files
Mulder stumbles on Monica & Chandler in a box and is convinced they are aliens. Or is he? Yes he is. Or is he? Yes I said.

8.30 Actual Proof of Alien Life
Andy Crane shows a film of a moving lamp and says 'lamp or not lamp? you decide.'

9.30 Furends
The one where Chandler is forced to marry Scully as a bet, but will Joey discover his arse?

Joey is worried that he is earning less than Monica who is earning more than Chandler (6pm)

10.0 Furends
The one with Russel Grant and Monica pretending to be insane to convince Rusty Lee they will make good cooks.

10.30 Filthy Screw People
A pretend-incisive look at the sex industry containing shots of a pair of breasts that look like old yellow balloons filled with clay and a very ugly nude man.

11.0 Furends
The one where Phoebe catches Ross and Joey upside down and wants to join in but Chandler has other plans and may or may not be gay! Of course he's straight really, and that's why it's so very funny.

12.0 Furends
The one, blah, blah, blah...

12.30 Ladies Of Nakedicity
Cockumentary about ladies who are prepared to take their clothes off for a TV programme. This one in fact. We see this. Possibility of wanking.

DR. FISCHER VERLAG'S PERSONAL INSANITY TEST

Every now and again, many of us find ourselves thinking the kind of thoughts or doing the kind of things that only an insane person would. Why not find out if you really do need professional help with my handy personal insanity test. Simply answer 'yes' or 'no' to the following questions, keep a count of the times you say 'yes', then check your result on the chart below.

1. At the cinema, do you like to laugh just before anyone else does?
2. Do you own any records by 'Phats and Small'?
3. If you leave a power point switched on with no plug in it, do you worry that the electricity is leaking out?
4. Do you think Gino Ginelli is really Italian?
5. Do you find fresh fruit sexually arousing?
6. Does Frank Bough ever pop into your head while you're masturbating?
7. Do you like the taste of marzipan?
8. Do you have any words tattooed on your face?
9. Do you find the smell of your socks fascinating?
10. Have you ever been to 'The Royal Tournament'?
11. Do you like wearing lots of badges?
12. Do you ever find yourself dribbling without realising it?
13. Have you been back to visit your old school more than once?
14. Have you ever considered going on a TV talent show?
15. Are you constantly grinning even though there's no reason to?
16. When at a theme park, do you get autographs from people dressed as cartoon characters?
17. Do you regularly watch 'The National Lottery Live'?
18. Do you ever find your eyes lingering a bit too long on dogshit?
19. Have you ever spanked yourself to see if you like it?
20. Have you ever bought a 'cassingle'?
21. Do you wish the news was broadcast in Surround Sound?
22. When you're at a gig, do you ever think the lead singer is singing entirely to you?
23. Did you think *Event Horizon* was an exciting film?
24. Would you walk more than two meters out of your way to crush an empty cigarette packet underfoot?
25. Do you think nuns are funny?
26. When you concentrate hard, does your tongue stick out?
27. Is your CD, book or record collection alphabetised?
28. Halfway through reading a book, do you realise you haven't taken any of it in because you've been thinking about something else?
29. Do you think your jokes are too clever for anyone else to get?
30. When listening to your walkman in the street, do find yourself walking in rhythm?
31. Are you up to date on the latest developments in Ginger Spice's career?
32. Do you like to 'shop around for the best deal'?
33. Do you find it comforting to have the TV on with the sound down?
34. Do you like how it feels to sit in a corner?
35. Do you like liver?
36. Do you enjoy pot holing?
37. Have you ever considered calling Raj or Denise on 'Richard & Judy' for advice?
38. Do you rather enjoy the sensation of mild electric shocks?
39. Have you ever tried shaving your nipples?
40. Have you paid to see Brian Conley in the theatre?
41. Has Robin Williams ever moved you to tears?
42. Do you think politicians know what they're doing?
43. Have you ever chewed your cuticles until your fingers bleed?
44. Has Robbie Williams ever moved you to tears?
45. Do you think exams are a good indication of intelligence?
46. Have you ever spent more than half an hour browsing in a video shop only to leave empty handed?
47. Have you ever seriously used the word 'unputdownable'?
48. Have you ever written to 'Ainsley Harriot's Party of a Lifetime'?
49. Do you know all the words to 'Evita'?
50. Do you look forward to getting things repaired?
51. Are you glad when a taxi driver strikes up a conversation?
52. Do you think about yourself when you're having sex?
53. Do you find yourself jiggling parts of your body very fast for no reason?
54. If you are a man, do you refer to your girlfriend as 'the wife'?
55. Do you indulge in lengthy fantasies about how devastated your friends would be if you died suddenly?
56. Do you spend so long getting ready to go out that you make yourself late every time?
57. Do you think attaching one end of cassette tape to a lamp post then driving away as it unwinds is the coolest thing ever?
58. Have you ever waved a piece of paper with 'TUNE!' written on it at the DJ in a club?
59. Do you hum along with the incidental music on TV shows or sing along with the songs on commercials?
60. Have you ever gone into a record shop and asked for 'the song from that car/jeans/beer advert'?
61. When someone says 'let's meet up for a drink sometime' do you get excited about it?
62. Do you like the taste of envelope glue?
63. Do you still fantasise about having special powers?
64. Do you read self-improvement books?
65. Did you get turned on when your Mum used to spit on a hanky and wipe your face with it?
66. Do you think Lenny Kravitz 'rocks'?
67. Have you ever thought 'I just can't get enough of this bogey'?
68. Do you have pet names for your body parts?
69. Do you like Red Bull?
70. Would you let Dr Fischer Verlag conduct experiments on you?

CHECK YOUR HEAD

0-10	You are sane but boring. Why not try doing some of the things on list?
11-20	Nothing to worry about, you're just a bit stupid. Try not to talk too much.
21-30	You are demented, but I like you. Let's meet up for a drink.
31-40	At first you seem interesting, but soon you reveal yourself as a nutcake.
41-50	You think you are fascinatingly individual, but actually you are an appalling loopfruit.
51-70	Stay away from me. Someone call the police, quickly.

'yes'

Wow! All the bits from all the shows. It's like a really big track listing, only for a non-existent video instead of a tape.

SERIES 1
SHOW 1
1. TOYTRAINSPOTTING
2. SHAKEYCAM LINK
3. BAAADDAD REVIEWS:
   Higher State Of Consciousness: Josh Wink
   Frank Black: Men In Black
   Ice Cube & Dr Dre: Natural Born Killaz
4. FREE STUFF ON MAGS LINK
5. 20% EXTRA FREE
6. CANDLE FIDDLES LINK
7. WAITERS GET REVENGE
8. CD'S ARE CRAP LINK
9. VINYL JUSTICE with Cerys from Catatonia
10. PLANE CRASH MONTAGE
11. LOUISE'S GUIDE TO LIFE: Urinals
12. PRODUCT ROUNDUP

SHOW 2
1. SEVEN DWARVES
2. STUDIO AUDIENCE LINK
3. BAAADDAD REVIEWS:
   Underworld: Born Slippy
   Chemical Brothers: Setting Sun
   Prodigy: Firestarter
4. CEREAL LINK
5. PEE PEE DOCTOR
6. NEWSAGENT vs INTERNET
7. FIGURINE PHYSIQUES LINK
8. STAR WARS: Chew've Been Framed
9. HAIRCUT 100 LINK
10. VINYL JUSTICE with Nick Heyward
11. LOUISE'S GUIDE TO LIFE: Parties
12. PRODUCT ROUNDUP

SHOW 3
1. SHOWTOYS
2. LITTLE THINGS LINK
3. US vs UK
4. VIDEO BOXED SETS LINK
5. LOUISE'S GUIDE TO LIFE: Videoshops
6. TAPE COMPILATIONS LINK
7. BAAADDAD COMMENTS ON:
   Peter Andre: Flava
   Louise: Naked
   The Spice Girls: Wannabe
8. SERIAL KILLERS MONTAGE
9. VINYL JUSTICE with Neil Hannon out of
   The Divine Comedy
10. PRODUCT ROUNDUP

SHOW 4
1. STAR WARS: Blind Data
2. NEW YEAR'S LINk
3. BAAADDAD COMMENTS ON:
   Pet Shop Boys: Se A Vida E
   2 Pac: I Aint Mad At Cha
   Baby Bird: You're Gorgeous
4. CAR JOURNEYS LINK
5. MOTORWAY SERVICES REVIEW
6. BAD BEHAVIOUR IN CINEMAS LINK
7. TOYKIDS
8. SPACE DUST LINK
9. VINYL JUSTICE with John & Euros out of
   Gorky's Zygotic Mynci
10. CRISP COLOURS LINK
11. LOUISE'S GUIDE TO LIFE: Walking Down
   The Street
12. PRODUCT ROUNDUP

SERIES 2
SHOW 1
1. THE TOY PATIENT
2. CAMCORDER FRAME WELCOME
3. BAAADDAD VISITS TRIBAL GATHERING
4. COLDS LINK
5. ROOM 4 CHANGE
6. CLEAN AND CLEAR AD SPOOF
7. KEN KORDA: pitching your movie
8. PRODUCT BEREAVEMENT LINK
9. VINYL JUSTICE with Gary Numan
10. FOOTBALL SONG

SHOW 2
1. SHINEY
2. 'THESE ARE TROUBLED TIMES' LINK
3. YOU BREAK IT, YOU PAY FOR IT
4. CIGARETTE PACKET FIDDLES
5. BAAADDAD REVIEWS:
   The Verve: Bitterwseet Symphony
   Radiohead: Paranoid Android
   Blur: Song 2
6. EXTRA FOOTAGE ON VIDEOS LINK
7. STAR WARS In Their Eyes
8. KEN KORDA: researching your movie
9. PLANE JOURNEYS GUIDE
10. VINYL JUSTICE with Ahmet Zappa

SHOW 3
1. EMERGENCY PLAY ROOM
2. VIRTUAL STUDIO LINK
3. BAAADDAD VISITS THE PHOENIX FESTIVAL
4. STREET ARTISTS INTRO
5. STREET ARTISTS
6. CD PACKAGING LINK
7. KEN KORDA: casting your movie
8. GIG GUIDE
9. VINYL JUSTICE with Edwyn Collins
10. FOOD & DREAMS LINK
11. WHAT DO YOU DO? SONG

SHOW 4
1. TFI A LONG TIME AGO IN A GALAXY FAR
   FAR AWAY
2. AN AUDIENCE WITH ADAM & JOE
3. BAAADDAD REVIEWS:
   No Doubt: Don't Speak
   Hanson: Mmmm Bop
   Chumbawumba: Tubthumping
4. RENT BOYS
5. CRECHE
6. KEN KORDA: the making of 'Needlebliss'
7. MICROWAVE TRICKS
8. VINYL JUSTICE with Symposium

SHOW 5
1. STUFF THIS LIFE
2. ADAM & JOE'S BIG MONEY GAME SHOW
3. BAAADDAD VISITS V97
4. PULLING A SICKIE
5. IN-STORE MUSIC
6. SUNRISE MOBILITY SCOOTER AD
7. KEN KORDA: editing your movie
8. CAMCORDER REACTIONS GUIDE
9. VINYL JUSTICE with Stereolab
10. VIDEO GAMES LINK
11. TETRIS SONG

SHOW 6
1. FURENDS
2. SPONSORED BY ADAM & JOE
3. BAAADDAD REVIEWS:
   Oasis: D'you Know What I Mean?
   Supergrass: Late In The Day
   Elton John: Candle In The Wind
4. VINYL JUSTICE with Dave Navarro
5. STAR WARS: Leia!
6. KEN KORDA: the screening
7. BEHIND THE SCENES LINK
8. PISS UP IN A BREWERY

SERIES 3
SHOW 1
1. SAVING PRIVATE LION
2. HEINZ INTRO
3. BAAADDAD VISITS: Coolio
4. DR SPANKLE'S HOLLYWOOD
   WAX-O-RAMA
5. STAR WARS: This Morning With Han &
   Chewie
6. REMEMBERING PEOPLE'S NAMES
7. VINYL JUSTICE with Mark E Smith
8. SONG: Robert De Niro Calypso
   (not real calypso)

SHOW 2
1. ALLY McSQUEAL
2. ADAM & JOE ALLIANCE INTRO
3. BAAADDAD IN IBIZA Part One: The Clubs
4. MIME ARTISTS
5. KEN KORDA FORMS A TEEN BAND
   Part One: The Auditions
6. GUIDE TO SHARING A BED WITH
   SOMEONE
7. RECORD STORE GUIDE Part One:
   The Dance Music Shop
8. VINYL JUSTICE with Frank Black
9. TOTTIES OUTRO

SHOW 3
1. SHAKESBEARE IN LOVE
2. OBLIGATORY FLAT ERIC SPOOF INTRO
3. BAAADDAD VISITS: The Chapman
   Brothers
4. SERIAL KILLERS IN THE HARDWARE STORE
5. STAR WARS: Chew Wants To Be A
   Millionaire
6. VINYL JUSTICE with Thomas Dolby
7. SONG: My Name is Roscoe
8. COMPUTER CRASH OUTRO

SHOW 4
1. STUFFED TREK: The Toy Generation
2. ZANY CREW INTRO
3. BAAADDAD IN IBIZA Part Two: Club 18-30
4. MASTERS OF DISGUISE
5. KEN KORDA FORMS A TEEN BAND
   Part Two: Recording The Single
6. THROWING SHIT AWAY
7. RECORD STORE GUIDE Part Two:
   The Record And Tape Exchange
8. VINYL JUSTICE with Mark Morris
9. RIGHT 2 REPLY/QUANTUM LEAP OUTRO

SHOW 5
1. TOYTANIC: THE DIRECTOR'S CUT PART 1
2. DISEMBODIED VOICE GUY INTRO
3. KEN KORDA FORMS A TEEN BAND
   Part Three: The Live Performance!
4. THE LAUNDERETTE DOCUSOAP
5. STAR WARS: Jedi Springer
6. VINYL JUSTICE with Alexis Arquette
7. SONG: Song For Bob Hoskins
8. HILARIOUS VOICE OVER PAY-OFF OUTRO

SHOW 6
1. TOYTANIC: THE DIRECTOR'S CUT PART 2
2. LAST EVER INTRO
3. BAAADDAD IN IBIZA
   Part Three: Manumission
4. GUIDE TO BEING A SHIT DRIVER
5. NEW NAMES FOR CONFECTIONERY
6. GUIDE TO TAKING A PEE
7. RECORD STORE GUIDE Part Three:
   The Megastore
8. GUIDE TO DEALING WITH THE COPS
9. VINYL JUSTICE with Ray Manzarek
10. 'NETWORK' OUTRO

OE'S THANKYOUS: All thanks 2 God/Love/Truth 4 Universal Knowledge, 2 my beloved parents 4 giving me life, 2 Puff Daddy & Zac Sandler 4 all their inspiration & in[...] you all always. ADAM (vocals, moog, drum patterns, atmospheres and hob nobs) THANKS: Dave for the good times and the bad times, Sel for making me believe [...] us whole. Together we have created a book that should last as long as a copy of the Bible. Peace.

I could fly and picking me up when I jumped out of the window, Zac, Lou, Mark & Ziv for the crazy, crazy nights, Mum, Dad, Clare and Rob for being there when things got just a bit too wild, Peter & Steph for

for weaving our vision into reality and Fenton and Randy for believing anything was possible and anyone else I have forgotten. You know who you are even if we don't. And of course, the fans. You make

this book possible, 2 Jonathan Ross & Jane Goldman for helping us keep it real through the madness, and finally 2 my beautiful Annabel, our boys Fron, Child & Cujo & our baby girls taboo and Mirage, I will love

duction work, 2 Clare Hulton, Dan Newman, Richard Evans, Jimmy Jam, Terry Lewis, Charlotte Glover, Dominic Saraceno & all at Boxtree who worked so hard 2 make

keeping the tabloids away, Anna, Toby, Matt R, Rob B, Adam, Paul, Mandy, Matt G, Louise, Jo, Annette and Debbie for booking taxis to and from The Priory, Jon